Vietnam and International Law

VIETNAM
AND
INTERNATIONAL LAW

An Analysis of International Law
and the Use of Force, and the
Precedent of Vietnam for
Subsequent Interventions

The Consultative Council
of the Lawyers Committee on
American Policy Towards Vietnam

Richard Falk, Chair
John H. E. Fried, Rapporteur

With a new preface by Richard Falk

ALETHEIA PRESS
1990

Aletheia Press
P.O. Box 1178
Northampton, Massachusetts 01061

Manufactured in the United States of America

Library of Congress Cataloging-in-Publication Data

Vietnam and international law : an analysis of international law and the use of force, and the precedent of Vietnam for subsequent interventions / the Consultative Council of the Lawyers Committee on American Policy Towards Vietnam ; Richard Falk, chair ; John H. E. Fried, rapporteur ; with a new preface by Richard Falk.

p. cm.

Reprint, with new preface. Originally published: Flanders, N.J. : O'Hare, 1967.

Includes bibliographical references and index.

ISBN 0–9623718–3–1 (lib. bdg.) : $27.50.—ISBN 0–9623718–0–7 (pbk.) : $12.50

1. Aggression (International law) 2. International law—United States. 3. Vietnamese Conflict, 1961–1975. I. Fried, John H. E. II. Lawyers Committee on American Policy Towards Vietnam. Consultative Council.

JX4471.V54 1990
341.5'8—dc20

90–36599
CIP

Contents

Preface

Vietnam and International Law: The Past Recalled and the Future Challenged

Against the background of an evolving system of international law and criminal responsibility for its violation, the Lawyers Committee on American Policy Towards Vietnam (hereafter called the Lawyers Committee) was formed in the mid-1960s by a group of lawyers whose inspirational core included William Standard, Robert Boehm, and Joseph Crown.

The Lawyers Committee was organized to frame a response to a U.S. State Department memorandum of March, 1965, entitled "Legal Basis for United States Actions Against North Vietnam." This memorandum was prepared by the government to justify the explicit extension of the war to the north in February, 1965, allegedly as a reaction to prior provocations by North Vietnam that, it was claimed, amounted to an "armed attack" on South Vietnam. (We now know from later disclosures, including the Pentagon Papers, that for several years the U.S. government had been carrying out a program of covert military operations against North Vietnam, and that policymakers had been seeking a pretext for openly expanding the sphere of warfare.)

The Committee prepared its own memorandum in response, which was inserted in the *Congressional Record* and endorsed by many of the country's most prominent international law experts. The government was sufficiently challenged to issue on March 6, 1966, an official refutation of the Committee's memorandum. In turn, the Lawyers Committee encouraged the formation of an expert body of academic advisors, called the Consultative Council, with John H. E. Fried serving as its rapporteur. Professor Fried's industry and dedication resulted in *Vietnam and International Law,* published in 1967 as a document of the Lawyers Committee with the endorsement and participation of the entire Consultative Council.

It is, of course, difficult to assess the impact of this document while the war was being waged in Vietnam. I think it is correct to say that it offered the most widely known and respected legal critique of the government's policies and strengthened the political will and sense of moral obligation of those in opposition, including members of Congress, young men being drafted into the armed forces, and the general citizenry. It gave legal impetus to the antiwar efforts of such groups as Clergy and Laymen Concerned About Vietnam, and especially to their volume of evidence of U.S. war crimes entitled *In the Name of America*, which was compiled under the research direction of Seymour Melman and published in January, 1968.

The government in those years had sought the mantle of law in support of its Vietnam policies, and was sensitive to the legal criticism of its operations by some of the most respected international law scholars in the country, individuals otherwise in the political mainstream. Although the Lawyers Committee directed its legal attack against the Vietnam policy, the implication of its attack was that the policymakers responsible for the American war in Vietnam were "war criminals" in the Nuremberg sense. Especially after the disclosure of the massacre at Mylai in 1969, the peace movement picked up this theme, insisting that the Vietnam War was a criminal enterprise, and that our highest political and military leaders were potentially indictable as "war criminals." So persuasive was this contention that it became virtually impossible for U.S. officials to speak in support of the Vietnam War on any university campus in the United States. Officialdom stood widely, if informally, indicted by its own citizenry, a political reality almost unprecedented in the history of warfare.

The legal challenge to the government's Vietnam policy was particularly important in the overall atmosphere of the 1960s, with its strong anti-Communist consensus. Especially in the early years of the war, before the Tet Offensive of February, 1968, it was politically difficult for citizens to question the principles underlying the commitment in Vietnam. American boys were dying in combat, the enemy was portrayed as pure Red, and those on our side were associated with "freedom." Early principled critics of the war were viewed by the mainstream as disloyal, as engaging in behavior verging on treason, or as dupes of Communist propaganda. All along, it was possible to criticize the war from pragmatic standpoints as unwinnable, too costly, or as a poorly designed tactical effort; but it was not acceptable to question the moral and political desirability of enabling South Vietnam to remain a distinct state and a bastion of anti-Communism in Southeast Asia.

International law provided critics with a principled basis for an overall rejection of the Vietnam War, a basis that enjoyed legitimacy in U.S. society. The concept of limits on the legal right of states to use force was initially an American project. It was the insistence of the United States that pushed through the Pact of Paris in 1928, also known as the Kellogg-Briand Pact, which was the first legal repudiation in treaty form of the right of states to use force against their enemies. It was the U.S. government that pushed for Nuremberg, and gave the outcome its authority as a precedent for the future, especially as expressed in the Nuremberg Principles, drafted in the early 1950s by the International Law Commission, the United Nations specialist body for matters of international law. Likewise, the United States was a founding Member of the United Nations and a leading architect of the U.N. Charter.

The 1960s were still close enough to World War II to make U.S. leaders proclaim their commitment to the U.N. Charter and its fundamental undertaking, the prohibition of aggressive war. During the Kennedy and Johnson presidencies, the U.S. commitment to Vietnam was built around the proposition that North Vietnam was committing aggression against South Vietnam, and that the role of the United States was to enable the Saigon government to exercise effectively its right of self-defense. In that sense, the U.S. government locked its policies into a legal debate that turned on the interpretation of disputed factual circumstances: Did the Geneva Accords of 1954, ending the French colonial war, establish a procedure for a unified Vietnam that was deliberately undermined by United States policy and action? Was South Vietnam truly a separate state, or was it an artificial and illegal creation of U.S. policymakers? Was the opposition to the Saigon government associated with the National Liberation Front genuinely based in South Vietnam, or was it a creature of North Vietnamese machinations? Was the role of North Vietnam in assisting the NLF in the south tantamount to an "armed attack" that gave South Vietnam, and its ally the United States, a legal self-defense basis for extending the war to North Vietnam? Did the extension of the war to the north, principally in the form of heavy aerial and naval bombardment, exceed the limits of self-defense that are based on proportionality—that is, on a response proportionate to the attack? The Lawyers Committee briefly responded to these central questions in a careful and scholarly manner, and in each instance undermined the U.S. government's claim of legality.

There is no reason to exaggerate the role of this international law effort to oppose the war; it was one of several elements in the peace movement, and certainly not the most decisive element. Clearly, the domestic debate in the end turned on costs and battlefield results. The Tet Offensive was a critical turning point in this regard, undermining once and for all the optimistic claims of imminent victory being made by U.S. officials. The international law dimension, however, was not irrelevant even here. It gave those with moral and pragmatic doubts further reason to distrust the Vietnam hawks, and in the end to shatter the sort of consensus required to sustain an undeclared war in a constitutional democracy. The Lawyers Committee and its principal publication, *Vietnam and International Law*, which was actively discussed in academic and government circles, lent credibility to the international law argument against the Vietnam policies.

Reissuing this document in the 1990s serves two main purposes. First, it contributes to the ideological struggle to sustain an accurate historical memory of the Vietnam War, thereby resisting the revisionist project of the radical right and, more recently, much of the mainstream, to present the Vietnam experience as a heroic chapter in the struggle for freedom. Second, and more significantly, reviving the international law critique of the Vietnam War at this time reminds us how little we have learned since the 1960s and how important it remains to oppose the new forms of interventionary diplomacy that the U.S. government relies upon.

It is crucial to realize that U.S. military intervention in the Third World was not just an outgrowth of the Cold War. True, the containment of Communism and Soviet influence made interventionism saleable to the U.S. public during the Cold War years; but the impulse to intervene was most directly associated with keeping the world safe for the expansion of capitalism. This impulse has grown even stronger in the last decade. Ronald Reagan's embrace of the market as a global panacea has now been reinforced by the disavowal of socialism in Eastern Europe and even in the Soviet Union. The Reagan years successfully induced the media to equate democracy with capitalism, and to accept as legitimate interventions in any society that was moving in a socialist direction, regardless of how diligently it otherwise respected the restraints of constitutionalism. In effect then, as the Grenada, Nicaragua, and Panama interventions suggest, the United States remains prepared to impose its political will by force on Third World countries, ignoring their sovereign rights of self-determination and independence, defying the procedures of the United Nations and regional organizations to resolve disputes peacefully, and exhibiting thinly disguised contempt for any obstacles placed in the path of its foreign policy by the precepts of international law.

The climax of this recent phase of United States lawlessness was undoubtedly its decade-long campaign during the 1980s to overthrow the Sandinista government in Nicaragua, a small and poor country badly run down by prior dictatorial rule under U.S. auspices. Using the varied instruments at the disposal of a superpower, including a well-financed mercenary army known as the *contras,* the United States mounted a military and paramilitary campaign of harassment against this progressive government, which was dedicated to the eradication of poverty and misery in Nicaragua. When its anti-Sandinista campaign was challenged in the World Court in *Nicaragua v. United States*, the U.S. tried to withhold the dispute on jurisdictional grounds to avoid legal scrutiny. When this tactic failed, the United States explicitly repudiated the Court's judgment that U.S. policy in support of the *contras* was a violation of international law.

It is hardly surprising that the Reagan administration defied the World Court judgment in *Nicaragua*. That administration was so hostile to international law and to the United Nations that it repudiated the Law of the Sea Treaty, which even most conservatives regarded as a favorable agreement for U.S. interests. What is surprising, and profoundly disturbing, is how meekly the mainstream media, even its liberal components, accepted this defiance without critical comment. And what is more, congressional opponents to the *contra* policies, despite enjoying majority support and the backing of public opinion, were unwilling to censure the administration for the illegality of its Central American policies or to insist that the United States was morally and constitutionally obliged to uphold the World Court decision. Both the media and Congress were willing to oppose Reagan on Nicaragua, but only on narrow, cost/benefit grounds that the *contras* couldn't win and that the venture was a waste of money.

These same critics had no trouble throwing resources and paramilitary assistance in El Salvador's direction. Despite the similarity of the battle lines, although the forces of reaction held the reins of government in El Salvador and depended upon (or could not control) the death squads, the liberals believed that the counterinsurgency efforts by the U.S. and Salvadoran governments could prevail, and hence, by this test alone, deserved unconditional financial and diplomatic support. This liberal perspective will often find intervention acceptable for the sake of imperial goals, provided that it can succeed and that the more grotesque features of the behavior of our allies can be disguised.

Policymakers often rely on deception and secrecy to achieve some administrative distance from the commission of atrocities—for example, by blaming the atrocities in El Salvador on extremist factions in the armed forces and police, thus obscuring the official connection to those atrocities. Only in 1990 did an enterprising journalist, Kathy Kadane, establish that U.S. officials in Jakarta had provided Indonesian army leaders with lists of members of the Indonesian Communist Party back in 1965, thereby contributing to what the CIA itself has described as "one of the worst mass murders of the twentieth century." The similarity between our policy in Indonesia and the U.S.-directed Phoenix Program in Vietnam has been acknowledged recently by William Colby, who organized the Phoenix Program in the late 1960s, and who later became head of the CIA.[1]

From Vietnam and Indonesia to Nicaragua and El Salvador, mainstream critics in the United States have more often than not resorted to pragmatic opposition to intervention and atrocity, an approach that has failed to provide policymakers with an incentive to avoid criminal adventures abroad that violated international law and the right of peoples to self-determination. More recently, the World Court decision in *Nicaragua* provided the general public with an opportunity to resurrect the principled argument against international lawlessness, but the distortion of important facts in the case by the U.S. press and mainstream analysts left little room for an honest and open discussion.

One of the solid successes of the Lawyers Committee and the use of international law by the peace movement in the years of the Vietnam War was to challenge the earlier notion that international law was part of the repressive side of world politics, consisting of rules and procedures made by and for the rich and powerful. There is no doubt that international law had earlier legitimized the privileges of the colonial powers; had provided "legal" protection for foreign investment, however exploitive; and had sanctioned the use of force by the West on behalf of its imperial interests under such legal rubrics as "diplomatic protection" and "state responsibility."

In the last two decades this sense of the role and nature of international law has been transformed; its basic identity in the war/peace area has shifted from serving the state interests of the Great Powers to preserving the well-being of Weak States and strengthening the claims of the citizenry against the state. This is an exciting transformation with great significance for the future of democracy, as well as for the relevance of international law to the conduct of foreign policy. The disillusionment with international law within official circles in the United States is paralleled by a growing enthusiasm for international law in the Third World, as well as among peace-oriented citizens in our own society and elsewhere.

It is encouraging to note that it was the Non-Aligned Movement that took the initiative that led the U.N. General Assembly to proclaim the 1990s as "The Decade of International Law." In this regard, the *Nicaragua* judgment by the World Court was a watershed pedagogic event, teaching citizens throughout the Third World that international law fairly construed was often on their side. Even within the United States the judgment had an inhibiting effect on the Reagan administration, making recourse to an anti-Sandinista invasion of Nicaragua less likely in the late 1980s than it would otherwise have been.

In a related area, many antiwar activists during the Vietnam War went on to discover the Nuremberg basis for their opposition to U.S. interventionary policies in the years after Vietnam. Throughout the 1980s there were numerous political trials in the United States in which the defendants contested the legality of U.S. nuclear weapons policies or interventionary campaigns and claimed their own *legal* right to resist, even contending that citizens have a duty to use nonviolent forms of resistance to overcome government policies they reasonably believe are being carried out in violation of international law.[2] Such uses of international law, given prominence by the lawyering of Ramsey Clark, Leonard Boudin, and Peter Weiss, and by the passionate activist commitment of Daniel Berrigan, Philip Berrigan, James Douglass, Shelley Douglass, Jean Clark, and their many associates, have had the effect of reviving Nuremberg thinking as an aspect of citizenship in the nuclear age. The principle being insisted upon is that the price of legitimate government is to acknowledge that every U.S. citizen has a constitutional right to a lawful foreign policy that can be tested by independent inquiry in a domestic court.[3]

Of course, we are still a long way from achieving these aims. Most domestic courts continue to evade international law challenges by excluding the argument on technical grounds, relying on the ill-conceived notion that foreign policy initiatives are "political questions" inappropriate for judicial scrutiny. However, impressive inroads have been made against this statist tendency to deny access to courts to individuals or groups representing civil society. Recourse to courts as a check on abuses of governmental authority, including the pursuit of an illegal foreign policy, is gaining political momentum as a reformist goal. At a time when economists are saying that it has become impossible to distinguish the domestic economy from the world economy, it should be possible to induce judges to admit that the reach of law does not stop at the water's edge, that the president is constitutionally bound to act within the rule of law abroad as well as at home. Extraterritorial regulatory claims in relation to drug enforcement and counterterrorism need to be complemented by similar constraints on interventionary diplomacy, including covert operations.

In my view, these projects for political reform are rooted in the struggles by lawyers in the United States to raise international law objections to the Vietnam War policies. The Lawyers Committee led those efforts in the 1960s, relying on the energies of a small band of impassioned adherents, substituting conviction and commitment for resources, and persevering despite vast efforts by pro-war forces that had guaranteed access to the media and unlimited funds. In this regard, it is important to read (or reread) the Lawyers Committee document *Vietnam and International Law,* both to remember what the Vietnam War was *really* about and to deepen our understanding of the analogous issues and controversies that challenge our sense of decency and citizenship in the 1990s.

Richard Falk

Princeton, New Jersey
July, 1990

Preface Notes

1. For brief summary of these disclosures, see "Talk of the Town," *The New Yorker,* July 2, 1990, pp. 21–23; cf. also the more circumspect account by Michael Wines, "CIA Tie Asserted in Indonesia Purge," *New York Times,* July 12, 1990.

2. See Francis Anthony Boyle, *Defending Civil Resistence Under International Law* (Dobbs Ferry, New York: Transnational Publishers, Inc., 1987).

3. For theoretical basis confer Richard Falk, "The Extension of Law to Foreign Policy: The Next Constitutional Challenge," in Alan S. Rosenbaum, ed., *Constitutionalism: The Philosophical Dimension* (New York: Greenwood, 1988).

Preface to the First Edition

It is unusual for a group of international lawyers to go on record to the effect that their own government is waging war in violation of international law. Such an act expresses the belief that the national interest is better served by complying with relevant rules of international law than by the conduct of foreign policy free from the restraints of law. It is a belief that is heavily influenced by the experience of agonizing wars in the twentieth century and by the sense of concern that arises when we contemplate a third world war fought with nuclear weapons. It is against this background that the Consultative Council of the Lawyers Committee on American Policy Towards Vietnam was formed and it is in the spirit of seeking a law-oriented foreign policy that the Council now presents a comprehensive analysis of the legal issues raised by the Vietnam War. The analysis documents the conclusion that the ongoing military involvement of the United States in Vietnam violates international law in several fundamental respects.

As students of international law we regard it to be a matter of civic and professional duty to point out that war actions of the United States in Vietnam violate international law. At this stage of human history it appears increasingly patriotic to oppose even one's own government when it embarks upon lawless action in foreign affairs. Lawlessness in the setting of warfare imperils the welfare of the entire world, including one's own society.

We are mindful of the imperfections of the existing system of international law and of the impossibility of putting a legal straight-jacket upon the makers of foreign policy. At the same time we regard the rules and procedures of the United Nations and of general international law to be the fundamental framework within which any fruitful foreign policy must evolve. Disregard of this framework has resulted in the deep American involvement in Vietnam, an involvement that appears already to be the greatest tragedy ever in American foreign policy.

Perhaps the American involvement in Vietnam has grown to be so deep that it would be an illusion to expect a change in American policy at this stage merely in response to legal arguments. However, the paramount need is to find a way to end the war at the earliest time and we believe that a public awareness of the requirements of international law will promote this objective. It appears that at no point during the gradual buildup of the involvement since 1954 did American policymakers manifest a sufficient concern about the compatibility of their actions with relevant rules of international law. If at any point such a consideration had been given due weight the momentum of mindless involvement might have been arrested. We want to avoid future Vietnams and we want to insist upon the relevance of respect for international law to the avoidance of World War III. It is in this spirit that we offer the Legal Analysis of the Consultative Council as a citizens' white paper and urge attention to its principal contentions and to the beneficial effects that would have resulted from a timely willingness to abide by the restraints of international law.

At this time of arbitrary international action arousing the hostility and consternation of men of good will the world over, it seems appropriate to remind our leaders of the long tradition of respect for law that has been part of the national pride of the United States. It was the United States that acted as the chief architect of the United Nations Charter. Our statesmen, more than those of any other principal country, emphasized over and over again that the future of world peace depended upon the willingness of nations, great and small, to respect the rule of law in world affairs. Every year since the end of World War II on Law Day the President reaffirmed the adherence of the United States to the rule of law at home and abroad. President Johnson has made these solemn proclamations during his term of office. The cornerstone of the Constitutional tradition in the United States is well-summarized by the honored precept that "we are a government of laws, not men." The international dimensions of this commitment were embodied in the United States Constitution. Article VI makes duly ratified international treaties "the supreme law of the land." Mr. Justice Gray in the celebrated case of the *Paquete Habana* wrote in 1900 for the Supreme Court what has been affirmed by many subsequent judicial decisions—that the rules of international law shall be applied in the courts of the United States as often as they are applicable.

Our commitment is to a realistic ordering of world affairs. But it is a new realism that claims to be responsive to the special dangers of military action in the nuclear age. This new realism regards the rules prohibiting recourse to force by nation-states except in the event of an armed attack across an international frontier as a better guide to national action than some self-determined calculation of when it is necessary to use military power to promote national goals. We affirm that respect for these rules includes an acceptance of impartial procedures for assessing when it is permissible for a state to act in self-defense.

Yet, too often, it would seem, lawyers *assume* that states do and should adhere to international law in their foreign relations. Another tradition, associated with the name of Machiavelli and widespread in its influence upon public thinking, tends to consider law to be relevant only to the extent that it is compatible with perceived national interests. In this latter tradition the emphasis is not on the necessity to *act* in accordance with international law, but merely to *justify* or *rationalize* action as being in accordance with international law. This is an essential distinction.

There is a well-established diplomatic pattern that leads governments, even the most lawless and cynical among them, to offer a legal argument in support of controversial conduct in international society. Even Hitler claimed legal justification of German aggressions, but such pretense did not, of course, imply any commitment to act in accordance with international law. The Memorandum of Law on Vietnam issued by the Department of State in March of 1966 is an example of the use of international law to justify controversial international conduct. Such a document, important as it may be for obtaining a clear sense of the legal controversy, should not be confused with either an *impartial determination* of the legal issues raised by the United States presence in Vietnam nor with a real *commitment of adherence* by the United States Government to the limits of international law. The State Department's Memorandum of Law is an adversary document belatedly issued in reply to criticism, principally those raised in a previous brief by the Lawyers' Committee. The State Department's Memorandum should in no sense be confused with an impartial determination of the legal issues. It represents the traditional effort of governments to offer an *ex parte* justification of challenged national conduct.

The next big step in the struggle to achieve a more durable system of world order is for citizens to organize themselves so as to be able to insist effectively that their own government adhere to international law. The world is both too small and too dangerous to allow each country to decide for itself when to use military force. If this lesson, or some part of it, can be learned from the war in Vietnam we may still be able to turn this ghastly experience to some positive use.

Richard Falk

Princeton, New Jersey
January, 1967

Foreword

The Lawyers Committee on American Policy Towards Vietnam was formed after the Department of State in March 1965 issued its memorandum, "Legal Basis for United States Actions Against North Vietnam." The Committee prepared a Memorandum of Law entitled, "American Policy Vis-a-Vis Vietnam," which, as far as we are aware, constituted one of the first scrutinies of the American policy from the viewpoint of its international and constitutional legality. The Memorandum was inserted into the Congressional Record by Senators Wayne Morse (Oregon) and Ernest Gruening (Alaska) on September 23, 1965 and was endorsed by eminent figures in the academic community.

Our Committee's original Memorandum, for the reasons therein documented, reached the regrettable but inescapable conclusion that the actions of the United States in Vietnam contravened essential provisions of the United Nations Charter; violated the Geneva Accords, which we pledged to observe; were not sanctioned by the treaty creating the Southeast Asia Treaty Organization; and violated our own Constitution.

It seems that our Memorandum and the wide response it evoked prompted the Office of the Legal Adviser of the State Department to issue on March 4, 1966 a Memorandum in an endeavor to refute the points raised by our Committee. That document represents the most detailed statement so far of the legal position of the State Department and of the Government as a whole with regard to the American involvement in Vietnam.

The State Department Memorandum appeared to us highly vulnerable and incapable of justifying an undeclared war of ever more fateful dimensions, and ever more serious implications. Mindful, however, that only specialists in the field of international law and international relations could prepare a detailed, documented answer to the State Department Memorandum, our Committee invited eminent authorities to serve as our Consultative Council.

With respect to the Consultative Council, it may be said that it represents more than a fair share of the most eminent, established and well-recognized academic authorities on international law in the American academic community. As a group, they are objective scholars without partisan commitment to any particular segment of the American political spectrum.

We are especially grateful to Professor John H. E. Fried who, as Rapporteur of the Consultative Council, assumed the main burden of preparing the text of the legal analysis.

The legal analysis of our Consultative Council emphasizes the obligations undertaken by the United States as a Member of the United Nations, and pursuant to other conventional and customary rules of international law.

This analysis is submitted for the urgent and careful attention not only of the legal profession but of all our fellow-citizens. As it rightly states at the outset, "This examination is not concerned with fine points of legalisms. At stake are the fundamental principles of world order."

We include, as an Appendix, the full text of the State Department Memorandum of March 4, 1966, in order to enable the reader to assess the official statement in justification of the United States course in Vietnam.

Lawyers Committee On American Policy Towards Vietnam

New York, N.Y. — William L. Standard, *Chairman*
January, 1967 — Joseph H. Crown, *Secretary*

Consultative Council

Richard A. Falk, *Chairman.* LL.B. (Yale), J.S.D. (Harvard). Albert G. Milbank Prof. of Internat'l Law and Practice, Princeton Univ.—Has served as consultant to U.S. Senate Foreign Relations Committee, U.S. Arms Control and Disarmament Agency, World Law Fund, etc.—Member, Exec. Council, Am. Society of Internat'l Law; member, Editorial Board, *Am. Journal of Internat'l Law*. Co-Editor, *World Politics*. Assoc. Editor, *Journal of Conflict Resolution*. Counsel, Ethiopia and Liberia, *South West Africa Cases*, Internat'l Court of Justice.—Member of New York Bar; member, Internat'l Law Committee of the Bar Assoc. of the City of New York.—Books: *The Role of Domestic Courts in the International Legal Order* (1964); *Law, Morality and War in the Contemporary World* (1963). Co-Editor, *The Strategy of World Order*, 4 vols., (1966); *Security and Disarmament* (1965).

John H. E. Fried, *Rapporteur.* Ph.D. (Columbia), LL.D. (Vienna). Adjunct Prof. of Political Science, City University of New York (City College). Previously, New York Univ.; Inst. of Social Research, Columbia Univ.; collaborator, Brookings Institution project, "Financing the U.N. System"; etc.,—United Nations expert on internat'l law (Legal Adviser to the Gov't of Nepal, 1964-66); Consultant (1950-51), Legal Officer (1952-54), United Nations; Senior official, Internat'l Labor Office (Montreal, 1944-47). Expert, Judge Advoc. General's Office, Dept. of the Army (1949-50); Special Legal Consultant, U.S. War Crimes Tribunals, Nuremberg (1947-49). Books: *The United Nations System* (Vol. I, Worldmark Encycl., 1963); etc. Co-author, *Annual Review of U.N. Affairs* (1955-1957); etc. Co-editor & co-author, *The Third Reich* (UNESCO symposium) (1953); co-editor (as the Tribunals' representative), *Trials of War Criminals before the Nuremberg Military Tribunals*, 14 vols. (1950-53).

Richard J. Barnet LL.B. (Harvard). Co-Director, Institute for Policy Studies, Washington, D.C.—Previously, Adviser on Internat'l Law, Headquarters U.S. Army, Europe; Special

Assistant, U.S. Dept. of State; Deputy Director, Office of Policy Research, U.S. Arms Control and Disarmament Agency; Consultant, U.S. Dept. of Defense; World Law Fund.—Fellow, Russian Research Center, Harvard Univ.; Research Assoc., Center of Internat'l Studies, Princeton Univ.—Member of Massachusetts and Federal Bars. Adviser, American Law Institute.—Books: *Who Wants Disarmament?* (1960); co-author, *After Twenty Years. The Decline of NATO and the Search for a New Policy in Europe* (1965); co-editor, *Security in Disarmament* (1965).

John H. Herz LL.D. (Cologne), Diplome (Institut Universitaire de hautes Etudes Internationales, Geneva). Professor of International Relations, City Univ. of New York (City College). Visiting Prof., Columbia Univ., Fletcher School of Law and Diplomacy, etc. Member, Institute for Advanced Study, Princeton Univ. Consultant, Rand Corp.; Political Analyst, U.S. State Dept. and Office of Strategic Services. Fulbright Fellow (Free University, Berlin).—Books: *National-socialist Doctrine of International Law* (Zurich, 1938); *Political Realism and Political Idealism* (1951) (This book received the Woodrow Wilson Foundation Award of the Am. Political Science Assoc.); *International Politics in the Atomic Age* (1959); co-author: *Major Foreign Powers* (latest ed., 1967); *Government and Politics in the Twentieth Century* (latest ed., 1965).

Stanley Hoffmann Diplome, Institut d'Etudes Politiques (Paris), M.A. (Harvard), Dr. of Law (Paris). Prof. of Government, Harvard Univ.—Research Associate, Center for Internat'l Affairs, Harvard Univ.; Associate, Kennedy Institute of Politics.—Books: *The State of War* (1965); *Organisations Internationales et Pouvoirs Politiques des Etats* (1954); etc. Co-author, *In Search of France* (1963). Editor, *Contemporary Theory in International Relations* (1960).

Wallace McClure LL.B. (Univ. of Tennessee), Ph.D. (Columbia). Advisor (1958-64: Consulting Director), World Rule of Law Center, Duke Univ.—Previously, Lecturer on Internat'l Law, Univ. of Dacca and Karachi (Pakistan), Duke Univ., Univ. of Virginia; member, Faculty of Am. Internat'l College, assigned to U.S. Air Force (Dharan; Dean, Overseas Div.; Prof., Bermuda).—U.S. Dept. of State 1920-1951 (incl. assignments at Montevideo

Conf. of American States; U.S. Legation, Stockholm; Ass't Chief, Treaty Division).—Member of the Knoxville, Tenn. and Federal bars.—Rapporteur, "The U.S. in the U.N.," Commission to Study the Organization of Peace.—Books: *World Legal Order: Possible Contributions by the People of the United States* (1960); *International Executive Agreements* (1941); etc.

Saul H. Mendlovitz J.D. (Chicago). Professor of Law, Rutgers School of Law, State Univ. of New Jersey.—Member, Executive Council, Am. Society of Internat'l Law.—Research Associate, Center of Internat'l Studies, Princeton Univ., Univ. of Chicago Law School. Visiting Scholar, Harvard Law School. Consultant, Harvard Grad. School of Education; World Law Fund; etc.—Member of Illinois Bar.—Books: *Legal and Political Problems of World Order* (1962); co-editor, *The Strategy of World Order*, 4 vols. (1966).

Richard S. Miller LL.M. (Yale) (Sterling-Ford Fellow), LL.B. (Boston), B.S. (Boston). Professor of Law, Ohio State Univ. College of Law; previously, Wayne State Univ. Law School.—Exec. Director, Detroit Internat'l Trade Conference (1963); Reporter, Michigan Juridical Conference (1961).—Member of Michigan and Mass. Bars.—Editor-in-Chief, Boston Univ. Law Review (1955-56).—Member, Regional Council, Am. Assoc. of Univ. Professors.

Hans J. Morgenthau LL.D. (Frankfort); Grad. Instit. for Internat'l Studies (Geneva). Albert A. Michelson Distinguished Service Prof. and Director, Center for the Study of Am. Foreign Policy, Univ. of Chicago. Previously, Univ. of Geneva; Prof. of Internat'l Law, Madrid; Visit. Prof. California, Columbia, Harvard, Princeton, Yale Universities; Visit. Research Scholar, Carnegie Endowment for Internat'l Peace; Washington Center, Foreign Policy Research.—Consultant, U.S. Dept. of State, U.S. Dept. of Defense. Member of the Missouri Bar.—Books: *Politics Among Nations* (latest ed., 1966); *Politics in the Twentieth Century*, 3 vols. (1962); *The Purpose of American Politics* (1960); *In Defense of the National Interest* (1951); *Scientific Man vs. Power Politics* (1946); etc. Co-author, *American Diplomacy in a New Era* (1961); etc. Editor, *Peace, Security and the United Nations* (1946); Co-editor *Principles and Problems of International Politics* (1950).

William G. Rice S.J.D. (Harvard). Professor emeritus of International Law, Univ. of Wisconsin Law School.—Honorary Member, Am. Soc. of Internat'l Law; two terms on Executive Council of that Society.—Lecturer on U.S. Law in Austria, India, Pakistan, Switzerland. Law clerk of Assoc. Justice Louis D. Brandeis; first General Counsel, National Labor Relations Board (1934); U.S. Labor Commissioner in Geneva (liaison with Internat'l Labor Organization); Member, National Defense Mediation Board; Asst. Gen. Counsel, U.N. Relief and Rehabilitation Agency (1945); etc.—Books: *A Tale of Two Courts* (1967); *Law Among States in Federacy* (1959).—Chairman, Wisconsin Civil Liberties Union; member of the Board, American Civil Liberties Union.

Burns H. Weston LL.B. (Yale), J.S.D. Candidate (Yale) (Sterling—Rockefeller Fellow). Associate Professor of Law, College of Law, The University of Iowa. Previously, Associate Attorney, Paul, Weiss, Rifkind, Wharton & Garrison—Member of the New York Bar.

Quincy Wright Ph.D. (Univ. of Illinois). Professor emeritus of Internat'l Law, Univ. of Chicago, Univ. of Virginia. Visit. Prof. New Delhi, Cairo, Ankara, Makerere (Uganda), Columbia Univ., etc.; Visit. Research Scholar, Carnegie Endowm. for Internat'l Peace.—President (1955-56) and Honorary member, Am. Soc. of Internat'l Law; Honorary Editor, *Am. Journal of Internat'l Law*; President (1949), Am. Pol. Science Assoc., (1950) Internat'l Political Science Assoc. (1944-46) Am. Assoc. of Univ. Professors; member, Commission to Study the Organization of Peace; etc.—Consultant, U.S. Dept. of State, Internat'l Milit. Tribunal, Nuremberg; U.S. High Commissioner, Germany, etc.—Books: *A Study of War* (1965); *The Role of International Law in the Elimination of War (1961); International Law and the United Nations (1960); The Strengthening of Internat'l Law* (1959); *The Study of Internat'l Relations* (1955); *Problems of Stability and Progress in Internat'l Relations* (1954); *The Causes of War and the Conditions of Peace* (1935); etc. Co-editor and co-author, *Preventing World War III, Some Proposals* (1962); etc.

I

The Unprecedented Character of the United States Involvement in Vietnam Requires the Most Rigorous Legal Analysis.

The actions of the United States in Vietnam are without historical precedent. Never before has any government intervened on a comparable scale in a foreign civil war. Never before has any nation, under the claim of collective self-defense, engaged in military actions of such destructiveness. Never before have military actions so imperiled the very nation initiating them—and all the nations of the world. For, the United States Government cannot give any confident assurance that this course will not lead to wider conflagrations, and even provoke eventually a nuclear catastrophe.

This policy increases the anxiety of the American people, among them, legislators and high-ranking military officers; it is opposed by many groups and leaders among the South Vietnamese people; and it receives embarrassingly scant support from the governments of other nations, their spiritual leaders and their citizenry. The Secretary General of the United Nations, the Pope and other religious leaders, heads of states, scholars and intellectuals, artists and writers, spokesmen for diverse national and international organizations and ordinary people everywhere—all have urged with solemn statements and appeals the abandonment of this policy.[1]

The stark aspects of the United States actions in Vietnam are relevant to legal analysis. It is common sense that the more a policy deviates from the normal and the more it entails hazardous repercussions and human suffering, the sounder must be its legal foundation. If a nation engages in a course of action that is destructive to others and dangerous to itself, the righteousness of such policy must be examined under the most rigorous standards. In international relations, just as in domestic affairs, the negative consequences of illegality increase at a rate roughly proportional to the size and boldness of the undertaking. Ever since the American revolution, the United States has acknowledged that a decent respect for the opinions of mankind requires that the causes that lead to momentous decisions should be declared, and that these causes must be just and proper.

It was only after a private group of American lawyers had, in 1965, questioned the legality of the United States military involvement in Vietnam,[2] that the State Department of the United States Government issued on March 4, 1966 a detailed Memorandum of Law entitled *The Legality of the United States Participation in the Defense of Vietnam*.[3] Since that time the war actions of the United States have continued with ever-increasing intensity in both North and South Vietnam and have also been extending to the demilitarized buffer zone. No separate official legal justification has been offered for this further escalation, and it may be assumed that the State Department considers the arguments set forth in its Memorandum provide adequate legal cover for events subsequent to its issuance.

The analysis that follows endeavors, as succinctly as possible and without claiming completeness, to examine the legal adequacy of the State Department Memorandum of Law. This examination is not concerned with fine points of legalism. At stake are the fundamental principles of world order.

II

Basic Facts About Vietnam

Shortly after the United States started overt war actions in North and South Vietnam in February 1965, the Secretary General of the United Nations, U Thant, said: "I am sure the great American people, if only they knew the true facts and the background towards the development in South Vietnam, will agree with me that further bloodshed is...unnecessary." (Press Conference, February 24, 1965).

A brief historical background of events follows:

a) A separate state or nation of "South Vietnam" has never existed. Before World War II the whole of Vietnam was part of French Indochina. During World War II pro-Axis French authorities in Indochina collaborated with the Japanese invaders. However, "the people of Indochina...resisted their Japanese overlords fiercely...led...by Ho Chi Minh, 'the Enlightened One.' The political organization which he headed was called the Viet Minh (League for the Independence of Vietnam) and consisted of a coalition of several parties of varying political views...Because of his resistance to the Japanese, Ho won considerable popularity."

b) "When Japan collapsed in August 1945, he...immediately proclaimed...a provisional government...The Emperor Bao Dai

abdicated his throne and called the people of Annam to support the revolutionary government of Ho Chi Minh."[4]
During World War II, the United States was "in the camp of the Viet Minh that was to become the Viet Cong; men like General Gallagher and Major Patti had hoisted the Stars and Stripes on the side of Ho Chi Minh and Giap [General Vo Nguyen Giap] in 1945..."[5]
c) "On March 6, 1946 a...convention...signed...be-tween the French Commissioner and President Ho Chi Minh...recognized the Vietnam Republic [of Ho Chi Minh] as a free state."[6]

d) Shortly thereafter, mutual accusations between the French and the Viet Minh developed into armed hostilities and eventually, into the bitter and protracted French-Indochina War (1946-1954). This "war of independence," as the Vietnamese termed it, caused heavy French casualties and approximately one million deaths among the Viet Minh.[7] During that war the French established a rival regime, the "State of Vietnam," with former Emperor Bao Dai as its President. France officially recognized the "State of Vietnam" on September 30, 1949. This was not meant to establish the separateness of *South Vietnam**, however, for the primary issue at stake throughout the eight-year war was whether the French-Bao Dai regime or Ho Chi Minh's regime was to rule over the *whole* of Vietnam.

e) The war went badly for the French, and in 1950 the United States formally announced that it would furnish "economic aid and military equipment" to meet "the threat to the security of *Vietnam*" not South Vietnam.[8] Secretary of State Dean Rusk testified before the Senate Foreign Relations Committee that the amount of American "aid" during the remaining four years of the Indochina War (1950-1954) was approximately two billion dollars. To most Vietnamese such massive, if indirect, participation made the United States an ally of France, a role that further prolonged the "colonial" civil war and made it even more bloody and costly.

f) By Spring 1954 the French military situation had grown even more critical, and on March 29, 1954 Secretary of State John Foster Dulles publicly proposed "united action," while acknowledging that this "might involve serious risks."[9] Thus the

* Unless indicated, emphasis in quotations has been added.

willingness to enter actively into the war was accompanied by a recognition of the fact that such action might ultimately involve a confrontation with the Soviet Union and/or mainland China. The proposal was rejected by British Foreign Secretary Anthony Eden and by Prime Minister Winston Churchill and his Cabinet because of Britain's determination to seek an end to the war through an international conference then in preparation.[10]

g) The Conference opened in Geneva on April 26, 1954 "in a mood of deepest American gloom [whereas] Eden felt that he had warded off disaster [namely a possible world war] and that now there was a chance to negotiate peace."[11]

h) Peace was negotiated, and on July 21, 1954 the Conference ended with the adoption of a "Final Declaration" which reconfirmed the independence of a single, united Vietnam. (The arrangements regarding Vietnam's temporary division into two zones for a two-year period will be discussed in a later section of this analysis.)

i) A few days before the Conference ended, France, in cooperation with the United States, installed Ngo Dinh Diem as Premier of the "State of Vietnam" that is, the Saigon regime that had been created by France with Bao Dai as President.

j) Between the latter part of 1954 and Spring 1955, the French gradually withdrew their forces from Vietnam, and the United States gradually assumed their functions, supporting the Diem regime in the south until its downfall nine years later in 1963.

k) The reunification of the two zones of North and South Vietnam, which was promised for July 1956 and guaranteed by international compact, did not take place. Instead, the United States resolutely maintained the regime of Diem and his successors, despite steady and increasing discontent and insurgency in South Vietnam.

To help a country defend its independence and self-determination may be deemed a noble undertaking. Indeed, the United States Government has attempted to persuade the American people that such "defense" against aggression justifies its presence in Vietnam. But the barest outline of facts indicates that the policy of the United States has been to *prevent* the self-determination of the Vietnamese people, to *prevent* the existence of a reunited and independent Vietnam, and to transform instead the temporary zone of South Vietnam into a separate country that is militantly hostile to North Vietnam.

This determination by the United States to maintain in opposition to the 1954 Geneva Accords a separate regime in the south has not only created an insoluble legal dilemma for the United States position. The manipulation of facts and issues appears even in the title of the State Department Memorandum, which asserts that the United States is defending "Vietnam"; and this obviously false assertion is at once contradicted in the Memorandum's opening sentence, which mentions United States assistance to the "country" of "South Vietnam."

The United States cannot and does not defend both "Vietnam" and "South Vietnam" at the same time. The United States is not defending the whole of Vietnam; from the beginning the United States has asserted that its central objective is to make the temporary division of Vietnam permanent and create a separate "country" of South Vietnam.

The arguments advanced by the State Department to defend United States policy in Vietnam are untenable in many other ways. They depend upon very questionable interpretations of fact and law.

III

The Military Intervention by the United States in Vietnam Violates the Charter of the United Nations.

A. The intervention is not justified by the right of collective self-defense.

Supporters of the United States course in Vietnam contend that the right of "collective self-defense" justifies intervention and that, in effect, the United States is entitled to respond to a request for assistance from South Vietnam. This claim is asserted in the State Department Memorandum to justify United States actions in Vietnam. To begin with, this contention admits that the United States is not defending itself against an armed attack by either North Vietnam or the Vietcong. They are not our enemies. Hence, under the Charter of the United Nations, and under general principles of international law, there could exist *only one possible* justification for United States intervention, namely, that the United States is exercising the right of collective self-defense. Indeed, there can be no other justification for using force.

One of the abiding Principles of the Charter of the United Nations is the obligation of its Members to eliminate the *use* of force and even the *threat of* force in international relations:

> Article 2(4): All members shall refrain in their international relations from the threat or use of force against the territorial integrity or political independence of any state, or in any other manner inconsistent with the Purposes of the United Nations.

The State Department Memorandum (Sec. 1, B) interprets Article 2(4) with curious superficiality. Calling this Principle "an important limitation on the use of force," the Memorandum creates a misleading impression. It is not a "limitation" but the keystone of modern international law. Threat or the use of force are not "limited"; in principle they are outlawed.

The Charter acknowledges that, for the very purpose of maintaining peace, various measures, and ultimately force, may be required. It confers the competence to use force upon the Security Council, thus making force the instrument of the world community, and not of individual states:

> Article 39: The Security Council shall determine the existence of any threat to the peace, breach of the peace, or act of aggression, and shall make recommendations, or decide what measures shall be taken...to maintain or restore international peace and security. (Articles 42 and 44 provide that such "measures" may include military sanctions.)

The essential meaning of this rule of international law is that no country shall decide for itself whether to use force—and, especially, whether to wage war through an intervention in a foreign conflict. Clearly, the United States, as a chief architect and signatory Member of the United Nations is, in principle, bound to admit that the Security Council is the only agent authorized to determine the measures required to maintain or to restore international peace.

The Charter does recognize, however, that grave emergencies may occur when an *immediate* military reaction may be necessary to prevent disaster. For these special emergencies, the Charter creates a very narrow exception to the prohibition of unilateral force:

> Article 51: Nothing in the present Charter shall impair the inherent right of individual or collective self-defense if an armed attack occurs against a Member of the United Nations, until the Security Council has taken measures necessary to maintain international peace and security.

This rule was most carefully formulated under the guidance of Secretary of State Edward R. Stettinius and United States Senator Arthur Vandenberg at the San Francisco Conference leading to the establishment of the United Nations. Article 51 constitutes, as has been emphasized by many international lawyers, the single *exception* to the keystone principles of the Charter and to contemporary world order—that is, the prohibition of unilateral use or threat of force. It is an accepted canon of construction that if a treaty grants an exception to a basic rule, such exception must be interpreted restrictively.[12]

The State Department centers its argument on the existence of this exceptional right of individual and collective self-defense. In justifying the use of force by the United States, the State Department Memorandum overlooks the relevance of a universal abhorrence of war, and the various steps that have, as a consequence, been taken to prohibit war as an instrument of national policy. Since the Kellogg-Briand Pact of 1928 the prohibition of war has formed a part of international law and has been accepted by the United States as governing the conduct of international relations. Seizing upon the reference in the United Nations Charter to the right of self-defense as "inherent" (that is, allegedly existing outside and independent of the Charter),[13] the State Department argues in favor of a doctrine of self-defense that did not exist even before the Charter and which, if accepted, would establish a unilateral right of military intervention and confer a competence upon nation-states to wage wars that might have the greatest consequences for the world.

B. The Charter permits collective self-defense only in case of an "armed attack." The existence of an "armed attack" is not established by the Memorandum.

The right of self-defense under the Charter arises only if an "armed attack" has occurred. The language of Article 51 is unequivocal on this point.

The term "armed attack" has an established meaning in international law. It was deliberately employed in the Charter to reduce drastically the discretion of states to determine for themselves the scope of permissible self-defense both with regard to claims of individual and collective self-defense.

Individual self-defense and, *a fortiori*, collective self-defense is not a lawful response to the commission of action unilaterally described as "indirect aggression," but only in the event that the victim state experiences an "armed attack," that is, if military forces cross an international boundary in visible, massive and sustained form. The objective of Article 51 was to confine the discretion of a state to claim self-defense to those instances "when the necessity for action" is "instant, overwhelming, and leaving no choice of means, and no moment for deliberation." In explaining Article 51, legal authorities usually invoke the classical definition of self-defense given by Secretary of State Daniel Webster in *The Caroline*.[14] Mr. Webster's description of the permissible basis for self-defense was relied upon in the Nuremberg Judgment in the case against major German war criminals. This judgment was, of course, based upon *pre*-United Nations law and, in turn, was affirmed unanimously by the United Nations General Assembly at its first Session (Res.95(I)).

There can be no disagreement with the assertion that "the principle of self-defense against armed attack is universally recognized and accepted" (State Department Memorandum, Sec. I, B). The real issue is whether the State Department's interpretation of what constitutes an "armed attack" has ever been recognized and accepted; or whether, in Mr. Webster's generally accepted words, the right of self-defense is restricted to instances "when the necessity for action" is "instant, overwhelming, and leaving no choice of means, and no moment for deliberation." The Memorandum relies upon legal authorities who themselves accept Webster's narrow conception of the permissible scope of self-defense, despite the obvious inconsistency between this conception and the allegation by the State Department that an "armed attack" upon South Vietnam has taken place.[15]

The correct delimitation of the concept of self-defense is not a "legalistic" question. The statesmen responsible for their nation's fate insist upon this differentiation between "armed attack" and other forms of hostile behavior; in fact, they insist upon safeguards to prevent unauthorized outside intervention in their affairs even in the event of an "armed attack." For example, the distinction exists in the Charter of the Organization of American States (1948) which in Article 25 differentiates unequivocally between an "armed attack" and other forms of aggression. The distinction is also found in Articles 3 and 6 of the Inter-American Treaty of Reciprocal Assistance (Rio Treaty) of 1947, in the North Atlantic (NATO) Treaty of 1949, in the Warsaw Treaty of 1955 and in the United States Japanese Treaty of Mutual Cooperation and Security of 1960—all four of these treaty instruments refer only to "armed attack" and make specific reference to Article 51 of the United Nations Charter. In particular, Article 2 of the Southeast Asia Collective Defense Treaty (SEATO) carefully distinguishes between "armed attack" and "subversive activities directed from without"; Article 4(1) of the SEATO Treaty covers "aggression by means of armed attack"; while Article 4(2) covers threats "in any way *other* than by armed attack" or "...by any *other* fact or situation which might endanger the peace of the area." This distinction is a crucial one. The question of life and death of many innocent victims of war may be contingent upon it—and perhaps, ultimately, the very survival of mankind. It therefore warrants the closest attention. The entire case of the State Department is based upon the premise that an "armed attack" by the North against the South has taken place in Vietnam. The Memorandum acknowledges that an "armed attack" must precede the exercise of self-defense and that indirect aggression does not satisfy this prerequisite. Astonishingly, however, the Memorandum neglects to document its conclusion that the alleged aggression amounts to an "armed attack."[16] It merely alleges the occurrence of an armed attack by North Vietnam "before February 1965," but fails to offer any evidence that such an "armed attack" occurred.

The State Department Memorandum quotes selectively from reports of the International Control Commission (ICC), created at Geneva to supervise the 1954 arrangements, to support its claim of subversion and infiltrations by North Vietnam. It fails, however, to acknowledge or to take account of the numerous passages in the ICC reports that criticize the forbidden, and progressively increasing, military build-up by the United States in South Vietnam that started almost immediately after agreement was reached at Geneva in 1954. It is in the context of this gradually increasing military build-up by the United States that one must assess the State Department's contentions regarding the infiltration of 40,000 North Vietnamese into South Vietnam over the eleven-year period between 1954-1965.

These allegations, even if taken as true—in fact, they are partially contradicted by many independent sources, including the

Mansfield Report[17]—indicate some intervention by North Vietnam in the civil strife or "insurgency" in South Vietnam, but they do not establish an armed attack within the accepted meaning of Article 51 of the Charter.

Contrary to the position taken by the State Department, externally supported subversion, clandestine supply of arms and infiltration of armed personnel were well known before World War II, and the statesmen at the San Francisco Conference were well aware of the history of long debates on the definition of different forms of aggression.[18] But the Committee chaired by Senator Arthur Vandenberg, which discussed Article 51 at length, purposely restricted the right of self-defense to a situation of *armed attack* because only these situations require *immediate* military reaction to avoid disaster. The rationale is persuasive: other forms of aggression, especially "indirect aggression," are so difficult to define and to ascertain, that too many situations might occur in which states, in good faith or bad, would claim the right of self-defense and thereby expand and intensify warfare. Any local strife could thus become internationalized by outside intervention. Evidently neither the Soviet Union nor the United States—to mention only these two participants at San Francisco—intended to allow a less precise definition of "collective self-defense" to grant each other the right to take unilateral military action whenever either state might claim to act as a collective "protector" of some government beleaguered by civil strife.[19]

The occurrence of an "armed attack" as the essential pre-condition for the use of force in "self-defense" is underscored by leading authorities on international law. For example, Hans Kelsen writes:

> It is of importance to note that article 51 does not use the term "aggression" but the much narrower concept of "armed attack" which means that...any act of aggression which has not the character of an armed attack involving the use of armed force does not justify resort to force.[20]

Kelsen examines a situation of the Vietnam type: State B "arming or otherwise assisting the revolutionary group" in a civil war in State A. States C and D construe this as "armed attack" by State B against State A and take war action against State B in "collective self-defense" of State A. Then "it is very probable that [State B] will deny to be guilty of an 'armed attack'...and might declare this action [by States C and D] as an illegal attack, against which it considers itself entitled to exercise self-defense."[21]

It is to prevent such developments that Judge Jessup argues against interference by outside powers in such situations:

> It would be disastrous to agree that every State may decide for itself which of the two contestants is in the right and may govern its conduct according to its own decision. The ensuing conflict...would be destructive to the ordered world community which the Charter and any modern law of nations must seek to preserve. State C would be shipping...war supplies to A, while State D would be assisting State B...and it would not be long before C and D would be enmeshed in the struggle out of "self-defense."[22]

Judge Jessup instead urges an "impartial blockade against both parties to the fighting." The 1954 Geneva Accords intended, as a precaution, something similar by prohibiting foreign armaments and personnel and military alliance and bases in Vietnam. The United States adopted an analogous stand-off policy, for example, during the India-Pakistan conflict in 1965 when each side charged an armed attack by the other.

Derek Bowett considers that restraint is legally *required*:

> ...the only proper course for states which are not themselves placed in the necessity of self-defense, is...to abstain from intervention...until such time as a competent organ of the United Nations has determined what measures are necessary for the maintenance of international peace and security, and what part those states shall take in these measures.

Mr. Bowett quotes the *Resolution on the Duties of States in the Case of Outbreak of Hostilities* (Res. 378(V) adopted by the United Nations General Assembly on November 17, 1950) which calls upon states engaged in hostilities to "take all steps practicable in the circumstances...to *bring the armed conflict to an end at the earliest possible moment.*" Mr. Bowett adds, "It is difficult to see how intervention by states generally could prove consistent with this end."[23]

The State Department Memorandum supplies most of the refutation to its own contention that an "armed attack" has occurred. Its description of the long-smoldering conditions of unrest, subversion and infiltration establishes a situation that is the very opposite of an emergency demanding immediate response, one "leaving no choice of means, and no moment of deliberation." The Government's argument, therefore, appears not only to be inconsistent with Article 51 but to deny altogether the letter and spirit of the Charter, which demands that states seek peaceful solutions wherever possible. This duty is expressed in Article 2 and elaborated in Article 33(1):

> The parties to any dispute, the continuance of which is likely to endanger the maintenance of international peace and security, shall *first of all,* seek a solution by negotiation, enquiry, mediation, conciliation, arbitration, judicial settlement, resort to regional agencies or arrangement, or other peaceful means of their own choice. (Emphasis added.)

The United States had ten years within which to seek a solution without resort to force, and South Vietnam was also bound by this same obligation. The reports of the ICC are full of complaints about South Vietnam's deliberate and systematic sabotage of the machinery created by the Geneva Accords. In addition, the State Department does not sustain the charge of external aggression by infiltration. It "*estimates*" that "by the end of 1964 North Vietnam may well have moved over 40,000 armed and unarmed guerrillas into South Vietnam." Even if this, admittedly uncertain and unproved allegation that these men came under *orders* from North Vietnam is accepted, the figure is not meaningful. Why should an unarmed Vietnamese who moves from one zone to another zone in his own country, be classified as "guerrilla" and "infiltrator," and provide the material basis for an accusation of "armed attack"? Above all, the State Department Memorandum conveys the unwarranted impression that 40,000 outside guerrillas had *accumulated* by 1965. The Memorandum fails to deduct all those who during a period of ten or eleven years died, became incapacitated, were taken prisoners, deserted, or simply withdrew from or never participated in the insurgency.

Furthermore, the Mansfield Report shows that before 1965, infiltration from the north "was confined primarily to political cadres and military leadership," and also notes that by 1962 "United States military advisors and service forces in South Vietnam totaled approximately 10,000 men."[24] The Report makes plain that a significant number of armed personnel were introduced from the north only *after* the United States had intervened at a time when the "total collapse of the Saigon government's authority appeared imminent in the early months of 1965":

> U.S. combat troops in strength arrived at that point in response to the appeal of the Saigon authorities. The Vietcong counter-response was to increase their military activity with forces strengthened by intensified local recruitment and infiltration of regular North Vietnamese troops.

> With the change in the composition of the opposing forces, the character of the war also changed sharply.[25]

Senator Mike Mansfield, in his Commencement address at Yeshiva University on June 16, 1966, declared:

> When the sharp increase in the American military effort began in early 1965, it was estimated that only about 400 North Vietnamese soldiers were among the enemy forces in the South which totalled 140,000 at that time.

To summarize this essential point—outside military intervention (collective self-defense) is permissible only in cases of a *particularly grave, immediate emergency*, namely an "armed attack." The kind of force allegedly employed by North Vietnam against South Vietnam cannot appropriately be regarded as an "armed attack" as specified in Article 51 of the United Nations Charter. Thus the claim of collective self-defense is unavailable to South Vietnam and, *a fortiori*, unavailable also to the United States.

C. Collective self-defense is primarily a right of the victim state.

The State Department Memorandum asserts that "Article 51 restates and preserves...a long-recognized...inherent right of self-defense." It implies thereby that any *outside* state has the right to intervene in foreign civil strife when and if that outside state, and/or the state directly involved, allege an attack. But this implication is unfounded. The very term, "collective self-defense," is not to be found in the parlance of statesmen or in writings on international law before the United Nations era. The term is not to be found, for example, in the Covenant of the League of Nations.

Writing on this issue, Hans Kelsen categorically denied the existence of any "inherent" right of intervention under the name of "collective self-defense":

> It is hardly possible to consider the right or duty of a non-attacked state to assist an attacked state as an "inherent" right, that is to say, a right established by natural law.[26]

And Julius Stone, whose writings are also quoted in the State Department Memorandum, declared:

> ...it may seem better to treat the term "inherent" as otiose and regard Article 51 as itself conferring the liberties there described. Thus, under general international law, a state has no right of "self-defense" in respect of an armed attack upon a third state.[27]

The term "collective self-defense" was first coined at the San Francisco Conference in an attempt to reconcile regional security arrangements with the existence of a new world organization. This interpretation was formally stated by Mr. Lleras-Camargo, the spokesman for the Latin American countries after the Vandenberg committee had hammered out the final formulation of Article 51.[28] It is evident that "collective self-defense" actually refers to outside military intervention—that is, to the internationalization of a local conflict. The Memorandum fails to cite any rule of general international law or to establish any precedent to validate the "inherent" right of outside states to participate in foreign conflicts. The absence of this "right" rests upon sound policy grounds. As the Vietnam case illustrates so decisively, intervention may lead to the destruction of the assisted party, as well as to the widening of local conflicts. Such an expansion of the scope of violence is fraught with danger to the international community as a whole.

Furthermore, the State Department's contention that, prior to the United Nations Charter, third states possessed a legal *right* to intervene by force in wars within other states is contradicted by legal logic, by the historical record and by solemn commitments undertaken by the United States itself. Logically, before the legal rejection of aggressive war had taken firm roots, international law and the practice of states tended to consider the parties engaged in a war as equals, and emphasized that third states were subject to the duties of *neutrality*; as such, they were expected to maintain a posture of impartial *abstention* from the conflict. This principle is borne out by the historical example of the colonial wars of the late 19th century. Also, when imperialist powers arrogated to themselves the right of intervention on humanitarian grounds, the "almost inherent" possibilities of abuse were warned against:

> It may be admitted that there are possibilities of tyrannical usage, barbarous practices, or persistent and hopeless anarchy, out of which friendly aid of a generous, impartial, and truly disinterested bystander

> may be the only way to deliverance. But two cautions must be interposed. First, it has to be provided that the aid is accorded at a time and under circumstances which do not in any way prejudge the issue of a struggle yet undetermined, and which ought, in the interest of the State concerned, to be decided by the real internal, and not by the factitious and external elements of victory.
>
> A second caution in respect to intervention is, that, admitting the propriety and duty of intervention in certain extreme crises, it is always open to a State, influential, designing and unscrupulous, to foster in another State, subject to moral control, the very condition of things which will, sooner or later, bring about a fit opportunity for its own overt interference...It is a danger which is almost inherent in the nature of the doctrine of intervention in certain emergencies.[29]

The view that wars of aggression constitute an international wrong crystalized at the beginning of the 20th century. However, the Kellogg-Briand Pact of 1928 does not refer to any *right* of third states to enter into a war on the side of an attacked state. On the contrary, the Pact stipulates the renunciation of war as an instrument of national policy, and the absolute obligation that:

> the settlement of all disputes or conflicts of *whatever nature or of whatever origin* they may be...shall never be sought except by pacific means.[30]

In the same year of 1928, the Sixth Pan-American Conference at Havana reaffirmed the principle of non-intervention for the Western Hemisphere. The International Court of Justice observed that the "resolute opposition to any foreign political intervention," as expressed in the 1928 Havana Declaration, constitutes "*one of the most firmly established traditions of Latin America*"[31]—a tradition which the United States accepted as binding upon itself long before the advent of the United Nations Charter.

Indeed, in 1933, the United States concluded a Treaty with several Latin American Republics which *specifically denies* any "right" of military assistance (which activity approximates the idea of "collective self-defense") on behalf of states in the Hemisphere that are victims of war of aggression. The Anti-War Treaty of Non-Aggression (Rio de Janeiro, 1933) stipulates that, if "*any* State" (even those outside the Hemisphere) were to use non-pacific means in any dispute or controversy against any party to the Treaty, "the Contracting States undertake to make every effort for the maintenance of peace...but will in no case resort to intervention either diplomatic or armed."[32]

To be sure, international law prior to the United Nations era did not preclude a state under attack from asking a third state for military assistance. But this is altogether different from the State Department's contention that third countries possess a discretionary "right" to intervene by force in conflicts between other countries. Even less can the Charter of the United Nations be construed as permitting a state to intervene in a distant conflict so as to carry out its own global policy:

> The Charter does not generally extend the right of self-defense to any state which desires to associate itself in the defense of a state acting in self-defense. The view that this is a possible construction of Article 51 is...based upon a misconception not only of the character of action in self-defense, but also of the whole system of the Charter...
>
> Moreover, to admit this freedom to lend assistance is to admit that states may, on their own initiative, assess the legality of another state's claim to exercise self-defense. This, it is believed, is entirely inconsistent with the whole plan of the Charter, which envisages the minimum of unauthorized action by individual states pending the intervention of the community on the authorization of a competent United Nations organ...
>
> Thirdly, this view distorts the concept of "self-defense" out of all recognition;..."collective self-defense" becomes assistance by one state, not itself possessing any right of self-defense, to another state which *may* [emphasis added] be exercising the right of self-defense. The range of individual state action, permissible without the prior authorization of a competent organ of the United Nations, becomes almost unlimited on this hypothesis. It cannot be a view consistent with the whole system of the Charter...It cannot be supposed that this extensive view of the scope of "collective self-defense" would ever have been accepted at San Francisco...[33]

In short, the right of an outside power to intervene in a foreign conflict under the title of military assistance is a *derivative* and *conditional* right: it depends upon (a) the right of the state directly involved to ask for such military action and (b) a genuine, *bona fide* request by the latter country. Neither the first nor the second condition has been fulfilled in the South Vietnam case.

D. The "request" of the "government" of South Vietnam does not provide a legal basis for "collective self-defense".

As has been demonstrated, collective self-defense is a right of the attacked state, not of the would-be protector state; hence, the importance of the principle that this right may only be exercised by an appropriately legitimate government in the event of armed attack. The equity of this principle is beyond dispute: military intervention, especially by a third state more powerful than both the attacked and attacking states, may have most unfortunate consequences. As the situation in Vietnam amply demonstrates, it may cause unbearable destruction in the "aided" state.

In view of the possible consequences of assistance both during and following the conflict, the government of the attacked state may not desire foreign military power to be applied against a neighboring state; such a use of force might, for example, make the attacked state vulnerable to further aggression by a protector of the neighbor.[34]

The request for aid can be justified legally, politically and morally only if it comes from a government that is master of its own decisions, and whose decisions with regard to directing, modifying or terminating the military intervention will be respected by the protector. In the case of a client regime, the initial request is but a formality enabling the patron state to intervene; the client regime will hardly be in a position to direct, modify or terminate the intervention.

This was the main reason given for the strong condemnation of Soviet intervention in Hungary in 1956 by the United Nations General Assembly and especially by the United States. Russia claimed to be acting at the request of the Hungarian Government under the terms of the Warsaw Pact, but this explanation was rejected because the General Assembly and the United States did not acknowledge the legal capacity of that Government to make such a request.[35] The present junta in Saigon, and its predecessor "governments," are appropriately viewed as client regimes of the United States; at no time have they been capable of making an independent "request" to their patron that represents the wishes of the Vietnamese people or fulfills in any sense the politics of national self-determination.[36]

Furthermore, the various regimes in Saigon have had a questionable constitutional basis and have not been able to obtain genuine support, even in those parts of South Vietnam that have been under their control. The continuing protests and demonstrations of Buddhists, Catholics, students, intellectuals and other groups are powerful evidence that the present regime of Premier Ky, like those that fell before, enjoys neither the consent nor even the acquiescence of the populace, and is not to be regarded as a genuine government.

There is overwhelming evidence that if the United States were to withdraw its military support, the Saigon regime would fall. Arthur Schlesinger Jr., former Special Assistant to Presidents Kennedy and Johnson, characterized the government in Saigon as "Marshal Ky's gimcrack bullyboy, getting-rich-quick regime," and called Mr. Ky "one of those Frankenstein monsters we delight in creating in our 'client' countries."[37] Is such a regime sufficiently constituted as a government to authorize foreign military intervention on its own behalf?

In essence, the State Department asks how anybody can deny South Vietnam the right to defend itself, or the United States to help in its defense. But this misdirects inquiry—the questions that really need answering are: Is the client regime of South Vietnam justified in requesting "protection" by an outside state in order to remain in power? And even if it is, is the United States permitted to assist a regime that lacks an independent will?

The United States acts as the principal in the Vietnam conflict: it proclaims *its own* war aims and determines the conditions under which it would, or would not, end the war or even permit negotiations for a peaceful settlement to begin. The fact that these war aims are extremely vague (for example, to "stem Communist expansion," or to "contain Red China") aggravates the situation by making it exceedingly difficult to pin down in advance what it is that Washington is trying to accomplish.

Even when United States military personnel in South Vietnam were acting as "advisors," President Lyndon B. Johnson stated that the war was being fought "*with our leadership and our officer direction*":

> We are going to continue to try to get them to save their own freedom with their own men, with our leadership, and our officer direction, and equipment as we can furnish them.[38]

The persistent debate in the United States about "escalation" indicates further that the crucial decisions are made in Washington. In this process, the right of the South Vietnamese to decide for themselves whether they wish further "assistance" is ignored by the outside protector.[39]

On March 20, 1966, the *New York Times* asked whether Premier Ky can "hang on" in spite of American backing. On April 10, 1966, the *Times* stated:

> Another possibility that the Administration faced was that a new coalition government might want to end the war by negotiating an arrangement with the Vietcong—an action now opposed by the Administration. But perhaps the only alternative to such negotiations, if Washington hoped to preserve South Vietnam as an independent state free of both Communist control and factional strife, would be open American occupation and rule of South Vietnam...

The same issue of the *Times* quotes the *Cleveland Plain Dealer*:

> American representatives in Saigon have been meticulous about avoiding any involvement in the present crisis but when the Saigon Government begins making moves harmful to the war effort the U.S. is going to have to intervene either openly or behind the scenes. A second war [meaning a "war" between southern factions] imperils the American effort and American lives and, as such, is not to be tolerated.[40]

Such statements, which reflect United States patterns of practice, emphasize that this is America's war. The claim that the United States is present in Vietnam at the request of the Saigon regime is also undermined. Such a "request" is scarcely adequate to justify the severe burden of war that must be suffered by Vietnamese people.

E.

1. The significance of the Charter provision that only "Members of the United Nations" may invoke the right of collective self-defense.

The United States military involvement in Vietnam is unlawful as there has been no "armed attack" against South Vietnam. It would even be unlawful if South Vietnam were an independent state and a Member of the United Nations.

Hence, even if Article 51 of the United Nations Charter did not limit the right to request military assistance (collective self-defense) to cases where "an armed attack occurs *against a Member of the*

United Nations," the United States legal position would not be improved. Therefore the question whether South Vietnam, as a non-Member, could nevertheless request outside intervention if armed attack had occurred is to some extent beside the point in the present case.

The State Department Memorandum insists that any independent state (whether or not a Member of the United Nations) and even a "zone" or "entity" such as South Vietnam, may request foreign military assistance. In view of the far-reaching implications of this contention, the meaning of Article 51 must be examined. In the expectation of eventual universality of membership, the wording of Article 51 does not intend to discriminate between Members and non-Members, but to prevent entities of insecure status from internationalizing local conflicts in ill-defined situations by claiming rights of self-defense.

On May 15, 1945, even before Article 51 had been written, Secretary of State Edward R. Stettinius, who headed the United States delegation to San Francisco, noted that:

> proposals will be made [at the San Francisco Conference] to clarify in the Charter...that the inherent right of self-defense, either individual or collective, remains unimpaired in case the Security Council does not maintain international peace and security and an armed attack against a member state occurs.[41]

Returning from San Francisco, the Canadian delegation stated that a claim of self-defense without prior Security Council authorization is only available to Members. The Canadian report commented that Article 51 "declares that a Member of the Organization which is attacked by armed force has the right to defend itself, and other Members have the right to come to its defense."[42]

Professor Julius Stone writes as follows:

> The kind of emergency justifying self-defense is limited by Article 51 to cases of "armed attack" against a Member, a far narrower and clearer formulation than under general law.[43]

The United States has itself previously acknowledged that the right of "collective self-defense" applies only if Vietnam as a whole becomes a Member of the United Nations. On September 9, 1957, arguing before the Security Council for the admission of Vietnam (not just South Vietnam) to the United Nations, Ambassador Henry Cabot Lodge said:

> [The people of] Vietnam...ask now only for the right to order their affairs free of alien domination and to enjoy the benefits of collective security, the mutual help which membership in the United Nations offers.[44]

2. South Vietnam was never considered for membership in the United Nations, and was not admitted as a Member of any specialized agency of the United Nations.

The State Department Memorandum concedes that "Article 51 is not literally applicable to the Vietnam situation" (that the wording of the Article forbids collective self-defense for South Vietnam) because South Vietnam is not a Member of the United Nations. But the Memorandum disregards its own acknowledgment by asserting that (1) "the Republic of Vietnam in the south...has been admitted as a member of a number of the specialized agencies of the United Nations" and that (2) United Nations membership was recommended for an entity called "South Vietnam" by the General Assembly in 1957 but prevented by a Soviet veto. These assertions are both untrue and highly misleading.

Regarding the first point, "Vietnam" was admitted to membership in the following specialized agencies long before there existed the temporary zone of South Vietnam: the World Meteorological Organization (WMO) in 1947;[45] the International Labor Organization (ILO), the World Health Organization (WHO), and the Food and Agricultural Organization (FAO) in 1950;[46] the UN Educational Scientific and Cultural Organization (UNESCO) and the International Telecommunications Union (ITU) in 1951.[47]

Hence, these agencies did not, and could not, admit an entity called "the Republic of Vietnam in the south" to membership. It is true that the Saigon regime has been *representing* "Vietnam" in these organizations, but this could not determine the existence of a separate state of "South Vietnam" any more than the fact that China is represented in the United Nations by delegates of the Taiwan regime establishes Taiwan as a separate Member of the United Nations.

Regarding United Nations membership, the General Assembly, on December 8, 1955 (Resolution 918 (X)) recommended membership for eighteen countries "about which no problem of unification arises," thereby excluding Vietnam. In January 1957 the Assembly requested the Security Council to reconsider the application for membership of "*Vietnam*"; the Assembly did *not*, as the Memorandum contends, make any request with respect to a part or zone of Vietnam called South Vietnam. Thereupon, on September 5, 1957, Ambassador Lodge, on behalf of the United States, asked the Security Council to reconsider the application of "*Vietnam*," and his draft resolution proposed that the Council recommend admission of "*Vietnam*" (although by implication, it is true that the presumption was that if Vietnam had been admitted it would have been *represented* in the United Nations by the Diem regime).[48]

3. An "international entity" called "Republic of Vietnam in the south" or "South Vietnam" has not been recognized by 60 countries.

The State Department Memorandum does not adopt the position that South Vietnam is a separate state; in fact, it indicates that South Vietnam "may lack some of the attributes of an independent and sovereign State" (Sec. I, D.2) and repeatedly refers to it as a "zone." The Memorandum incongruously contends that South Vietnam can nevertheless ask for outside military intervention on the same basis as would a Member of the United Nations (Sec. I, D.1):

> The Republic of Vietnam in the south has been recognized as a separate international entity by approximately 60 governments the world over.

The statement is untrue and highly misleading. The United States has never recognized South Vietnam, under the name of "Republic of Vietnam in the south" or by any other name, as a state or entity: at the same time as Great Britain, the United States recognized (the whole of) "Vietnam" on February 7, 1950, four and a half years before Vietnam was divided into two zones.[49] Many other governments recognized the state of "Vietnam" long before its temporary partition in July 1954. Before and after July 1954, the United States and many other states accorded diplomatic recognition only to the Saigon regime and withheld it from the Hanoi regime. It is true that some states established diplomatic relations with Saigon after the partition under the name of "Republic of Vietnam." This fact does not necessarily support Saigon's claim to be the legitimate government for the whole of Vietnam. Recognition does not establish the political identity of an area, and it cannot, of course, determine the geographic extent of a government's jurisdiction. The fact that 60 governments allegedly maintain diplomatic relations with Saigon does not by itself legitimate the Ky junta; nor does, on the other side, the establishment of missions in eight or nine countries of the world[50] by that regime's adversary, the National Liberation Front (NLF), make the Front "the government" of South Vietnam. Moreover, it cannot be presumed that 60 governments—including, for example, Great Britain, which is still the co-Chairman of the Geneva Conference—intend, by maintaining diplomatic relations with Saigon, to repudiate the Geneva Accords of 1954 that reasserted the unity of Vietnam.

4. Are non-Members of the United Nations without legal protection?

The State Department Memorandum asks the rhetorical question—are non-Members of the United Nations (including entities that are zones in a temporarily divided country) deprived of any legal right to act in self-defense? Non-Member states are legally entitled to the rights of self-defense, but the Charter requires that the United Nations determine when, if at all, it is appropriate to enlarge individual self-defense to collective self-defense. The point is that the United States, in the absence of explicit authorization by the United Nations, is legally precluded from acting in collective self-defense of South Vietnam; if South Vietnam had been a Member, then collective self-defense would be legitimate, provided only that a prior armed attack had occurred.

During the Suez Crisis, which involved overt military action against a Member state, President Dwight D. Eisenhower said:

> The United Nations is alone charged with the responsibility of securing the peace in the Middle East and throughout the world.[51]

And Secretary of State Dulles characterized as "unthinkable" a proposal that the United States and the Soviet Union act jointly to restore the peace in that area:

> Any intervention by the United States and/or Russia, or any other action, except by a duly constituted United Nations peace force would be counter to everything the General Assembly and the Secretary General of the United Nations were charged by the Charter to do in order to secure a United Nations policed Cease Fire.[52]

Article 51 does not render non-Members helpless in the event of an armed attack. It must be read within the overall context of the Charter. Article 35 of the Charter authorizes Members and non-Members to bring "*any*" dispute before the Security Council and the General Assembly. Thus, any Member may bring "any situation" involving a non-Member, even before such situation may cause international friction and before it may develop into a "dispute," to the Security Council or the General Assembly. The Security Council can, whenever there is any potential danger for a non-Member, proceed in a variety of manners (Articles 34, 36-42, 48-50); for example, it can order or authorize "preventive or enforcement measures" (Article 50) on behalf of non-Members.

Only after providing all these safeguards for non-Members[53] does Article 51 limit the right of self-defense (which, in effect, means *war* without prior United Nations authorization) to states that have passed the test of membership and have accepted its obligations. This Charter limitation guards against acts of aggression being disguised as exercises of the right of self-defense and prevents the internationalization of local conflicts by "entities" of controversial status soliciting outside military intervention. Nevertheless, in the early period of United Nations history, it was urged with some persuasiveness that, in spite of the clear language of Article 51, self-defense in the extreme emergency of armed attack must also be available to the many states that were not yet Members of the United Nations.[54] It is now being asserted that the clear words of Article 51—"against a Member"—must be ignored to avoid discrimination against the few remaining non-Members. Otherwise, states (entities) such as Switzerland, West and East Germany and South and North Korea would be deprived altogether of a right of self-defense. Such a line of analysis is misleading.

Switzerland, in deference to her traditional neutrality and after thorough debate of these issues, decided not to join the United Nations. Switzerland chose instead to rely on a combination of her own military capabilities (that had discouraged even Hitler from attacking) and on the Charter's safeguards for non-Members in the extremely unlikely event of an armed attack. Regarding divided Germany (an ex-enemy state), the Charter does not regulate self-defense as between the two zones. After considerable debate, first the NATO Treaty and then the Warsaw Pact have elaborately provided for collective defense against armed attack for West and East Germany respectively. This pattern of claims may be considered an evolutionary development in the meaning of the Charter[55] (similar to gradually changing interpretations of the Constitution of the United States). Its legal relevance arises from mutual acquiescence and acceptance by both sides concerned with the security of Germany. An armed attack upon South or North Korea would bring the respective provisions of the Korean Armistice Agreement into play. Therefore, Korea is protected by a special compact signed by all parties concerned with Korea.

This leaves only two non-Members of the United Nations: the temporary zones of South and North Vietnam (recalling that "China" is a representation rather than a membership issue). They were declared by special international compact (the Geneva Declaration of 1954) to form a single country even while temporarily divided into regroupment zones. Vietnam as a whole was neutralized by international guarantee. Hence, the legal and factual situation in Vietnam is altogether different from that of the other non-Members of the United Nations.

In spite of the strict wording of Article 51 we do not argue that non-Members of the United Nations, if they are sovereign states or well-established international entities, are deprived of the right of self-defense by the Charter. The relevant question is whether, even granting the widest possible interpretation of self-defense under both the Charter and general international law, a regime that does not possess political autonomy within its own society enjoys a legal right to request military assistance from a foreign country. The consequence of conferring such a right, as has been evident from the course of events in South Vietnam, is to allow a regime to obtain military intervention against its own people. In the Vietnamese setting such a right also contradicts the expectations of neutralization created at Geneva in 1954. If such a right must be denied, as we contend that it must, then there is no acceptable basis upon which the Saigon regime may make a request to an outside state for "collective" self-defense.

Considering the prospect of civil disorders, rebellions and *coups d'etat* throughout the world, the wisdom of the Charter in limiting "collective self-defense" to United Nations Members, or at least to truly sovereign "states," becomes apparent. The State Department Memorandum, "reasoning *by analogy*" and taking Article 51 "as an *appropriate guide*...in a case like Vietnam," contends that United

States actions there are appropriate. It would be disastrous for world peace if, "by analogy" any country, near or far, were allowed to intervene militarily on behalf of quarreling factions or "entities" of dubious status. For example, under this doctrine of interpretation Paris might well have been bombed into oblivion during the French-Algerian war of independence in the 1950s, since the Arab states and Communist China, recognizing the provisional government of the insurgent NLF, could have acted *as of right* at that government's request. Moreover, any foreign government would be justified in bombing the United States whenever the United States directly or indirectly intervened against insurgent groups that enjoyed some diplomatic status.

As has been shown, even though South Vietnam is not a state and not a United Nations Member, the rejection of such doctrine does not leave South Vietnam exposed to an armed attack or other hostile action. It has had available for its protection not only the ample safeguards afforded to non-Members by the Charter, but also the extraordinarily elaborate special arrangements of the Geneva Accords. But South Vietnam chose instead, with the guidance of the United States, to disregard all of these safeguards and to pursue unilaterally a policy of force in circumvention of the United Nations Charter and of the machinery created by the Geneva Accords.

IV

The Military Intervention by the United States in Vietnam Violates the Geneva Accords of 1954.

While the Charter of the United Nations, as the most comprehensive basis of world legal order, is of course applicable to the Vietnam situation, the particular situation in Vietnam is governed by a series of special compacts, namely, the Geneva Accords of 1954. Under a general principle of law, special compacts prevail over general rules, insofar as they do not violate them in letter or spirit. The Geneva Accords, carefully designed to restore peace to a war-torn area, fulfill the highest aim of the Charter. Therefore, as the State Department Memorandum recognizes, the legality of the United States course of action must also be scrutinized in the light of the Geneva Accords.

Regarding Vietnam, the Geneva settlement contains two salient features: (a) the unconditional guarantee that unification of the two temporary zones of the north and south would be accomplished through nation-wide elections to be held in July 1956; and (b) the unconditional prohibition of any foreign military build-up, including the establishment of any military alliance or foreign base. It must be emphasized that the latter provisions amounted to a *neutralization* of Vietnam, underwritten, *inter alia*, by the United States,[56] the United Kingdom, the Soviet Union and the People's Republic of China. In other words, the Geneva Accords go beyond the Charter's prohibition of the threat or use of force; to the extent that the governments of Vietnam were prohibited from obtaining outside military aid, the Accords *demilitarized* Vietnam.

A. South Vietnam was not justified in preventing the 1956 elections for unification, as prescribed by the 1954 Geneva Accords.

1. The Geneva Accords guarantee independence and unity to Cambodia, Laos, and Vietnam, and do not permit dismemberment of any of these nations.

It is often overlooked that the Geneva Accords "restore[d] peace in Indochina" as a whole, that is, in Cambodia, Laos and Vietnam. In the night of July 20/21, 1954, the French signed three armistice agreements: with Cambodia, represented by Cambodia's Foreign Minister, and with Laos and Vietnam, represented by the Viet Minh. During the afternoon of July 21, the multi-nation Conference adopted its "Final Declaration," which summarizes, guarantees and elaborates on these Agreements.

That Declaration states unambiguously (Article 2) that:

> The Conference expresses its satisfaction at the ending of hostilities in Cambodia, Laos, and Vietnam; the Conference expresses its conviction that the execution of the provisions set out in the present Declaration and in the [three] Agreements on cessation of hostilities will permit Cambodia, Laos and Vietnam henceforth to play their part, in full independence and sovereignty in the peaceful community of nations.

The only difference between the arrangements for Cambodia, Laos and Vietnam was the specific agreement concerning Vietnam for a *transition period*, unconditionally limited to two years: during the first half of that transition period, the French and Viet Minh forces were to regroup, respectively, to the north and south of a "provisional military demarcation line"[57] established at the 17th parallel (Articles 1 and 2). During the second year, "from July 20,

1955, onwards...the competent representative authorities of the two zones" were to agree on the modalities of general, nation-wide elections by secret ballot for the *unification* of the two temporary zones. These elections were to be held unconditionally "in July 1956" (Article 7).

The Declaration demands "respect for the independence and sovereignty, unity and territorial integrity of Cambodia, Laos and Vietnam" from the outset (Article 11); but this provision was applicable to Vietnam only as of July 1956. The point is clearly underscored in Article 6:

> The Conference recognizes that the essential purpose of the Agreement relating to Vietnam is to settle military questions with a view to ending [military] hostilities and that the military demarcation line is provisional and should not in any way be interpreted as constituting a political or territorial boundary.

As is generally recognized, the two-year transition period and the obligation to withdraw behind the 17th parallel was accepted by the Viet Minh under Soviet and Chinese pressure and constituted a considerable concession by the Viet Minh High Command; the formulation of Article 6, quoted above, clearly indicates recognition of the bitterness of the preceding eight-year war and the eventual possibility of new hostilities erupting. However, both the French and the Vietnam People's Republic properly withdrew to their respective sides of the 17th parallel, as attested to by the ICC.[58] The French and Viet Minh thus carried out their part of the bargain; the unanswered "military questions," which temporarily divided Vietnam into two zones, were settled well within the stipulated 300-day deadline, and on July 20, 1955, consultations between the two zones about the "political questions" (elections looking toward reunification) were to start. But at that point, Diem defiantly declared that he would not even begin *consultations*. Violent demonstrations in Saigon—permitted, if not instigated, by his regime—broke out against the Geneva Agreement and even against the personnel of the ICC.[59]

The State Department Memorandum endorses Diem's refusal to consult on the modalities of the elections, and thus approves of his action taken to prevent the elections and to hinder unification of the two zones. The Memorandum also raises tentatively the "question whether South Vietnam was bound by these election provisions."

2. South Vietnam is bound by the election provisions of the Geneva Accords.

South Vietnam (more precisely, the "State of Vietnam," as France styled the whole of Vietnam) was then still within the French Union as one of the Associated States of Indochina. The Armistice Agreement for Vietnam was signed on behalf of the French Union Forces, that is, on behalf of France. The Agreement specifically made not only "the signatories" but also "their *successors* in their functions...responsible for ensuring the observance and enforcement of the terms and provisions thereof" (Article 27).

Any implication that South Vietnam might not be bound by the Geneva Accords would render untenable the basic United States position that North Vietnam is bound by them. In this event, North Vietnam would be bound only if North Vietnam had agreed to fulfill obligations in the face of an understanding that the regime in Saigon was not similarly bound. This is evidently not the case. It is impossible to believe that Hanoi would have accepted an agreement that it knew to be meaningless, since the successor of the French, whose compliance was essential for ending the transitional division of the country, would be legally free not to end it. There would have been no *quid pro quo*: Hanoi would be bound by the Accords, whereas Saigon would be able to reap all advantages of the Accords, but free to disregard its own obligations, especially the keystone of the settlement, participation in the nation-wide elections for unification.

The only other conclusion possible would be that, in view of Diem's refusal to be bound by the Accords, these Accords did actually not come into being because, contrary to the appearances at Geneva, there was no agreement. In this case, of course, the Accords would be void and no party could be accused of a violation; hence, the United States could not justify its own action or South Vietnam's policies by alleging violations by North Vietnam.

3. South Vietnam was not justified in violating these provisions.

The State Department Memorandum does not pursue the proposition that South Vietnam was not legally bound by the Geneva election provisions; instead, it submits that South Vietnam's "failure to engage in consultations in 1955, with a view to holding elections in 1956" was justified because "the conditions in North Vietnam during the period were such as to make impossible any free and meaningful expression of popular will," and that in October 1956, even the Defense Minister of North Vietnam acknowledged the use of suppressive methods by the police. Such methods in the north cannot be condoned in the least, but it is clear that similar police methods prevailed also in the south. For example, the ICC Reports of that period (Sixth Report, para. 21; Seventh Report, para. 19) refer to Diem's General Order No. 6 of January 11, 1956, which "gave special powers to the Government to take extraordinary measures for detention or deportation for reasons of public security." The fact is that such "extraordinary measures" consisted of the creation of concentration camps.[60] It is noteworthy that the ICC Reports contain many more complaints about violations of democratic freedoms in the south than in the north.[61]

However, legally and in fact, disregard for democratic freedoms in either zone could not entitle the other regime to refuse even to plan and consult about the elections for unification. The Geneva Accords provided an entire year (July 1955-July 1956), during which time the two regimes were to engage in obligatory consultations to decide on the modalities of these elections; South Vietnam would have been at liberty to demand whatever safeguards it considered necessary for proper elections.

This opportunity to negotiate by itself defeats the claim that South Vietnam was entitled to foreclose these consultations. Such a claim also overlooks several other basic points:

a) that the Geneva Conference itself was aware of the need to safeguard the fairness of these nation-wide elections, and the Final Declaration (Article 7) stipulated therefore that elections would be held under international supervision;[62]

b) that from the outset of its existence the Diem regime vehemently opposed holding elections;

c) that the United States Government backed this attitude of Diem. As the State Department Memorandum (Sec. III, C) itself implies, the United States succeeded to the rights and obligations of the French, because otherwise the introduction of United States military personnel, arms and equipment would have been clearly unlawful under Article 16 and 17 of the Cease-Fire Agreement, even as "replacement." Thus, the United States is estopped from denying that it is a "successor" to France pursuant to Article 27 of the Agreement. To the extent that the United States encouraged Diem to sabotage the 1956 elections, the United States itself violated the Accords;

d) that the true reason for the United States and Diem to prevent the elections was the expectation that, even under all safeguards for free expression of opinion, the elections would have led to the downfall of the Diem regime;[63]

e) that neither the ICC, nor Great Britain and the Soviet Union as the co-Chairmen of the Geneva Conference, condoned South Vietnam's prevention of the unification elections; on the contrary, they insisted on holding both the consultations and the elections.[64]

The ICC continually insisted that the election provisions had not become obsolete through the passage of time. For example, its Eleventh Report (dated September 18, 1961, para. 88) states:

> Once again, during the period under report, there has been no progress in regard to the political settlement envisaged in the Final Declaration of the Geneva Conference. No consultations have been held by the parties with a view to holding free nation-wide elections leading to the reunification of the country...[65]

f) that the entire policy of the United States, ever since 1954, has been aimed at perpetuating a separate South Vietnam and that, because the anti-Diem outcome of the unification elections was virtually certain, their prevention became part of that policy. The policy also involved the systematic military build-up of South Vietnam by the United States, in contravention of the Geneva Accords. It is hard to see why a regime that would most probably come to an end within two years would require a military build-up that could not possibly be completed within such period. In fact, it would have been difficult to make Diem's "state" viable by the time of the election:

> In the aftermath of Geneva, the area south of the 17th parallel was in a state of political chaos bordering on anarchy...Diem...had only the shell of a government, no competent civil service and a far from trustworthy army.[66]

This determination to maintain a separate South Vietnam in spite of all obstacles has been often and authoritatively stated by officials in the United States Government. Two statements will serve as illustrations. First, Secretary of State Dean Rusk, at the ninth SEATO Council of Ministers meeting, April 13, 1964, said:

> As you will recall, in 1954 Vietnam had just been partitioned and the prospects for the fledgling Republic of South Vietnam were far from promising.[67]

The task that the United States set itself was described by Senator Nelson during the debate on the joint Congressional Gulf of Tonkin Resolution in August 1964:

> ...our mission or objective in South Vietnam...for 10 years [since 1954]...has been to aid in the *establishment* of a viable, *independent regime*...I did not suggest that by the use of hindsight I would now [1964] conclude that the [United States] intervention of 1954 [in South Vietnam] was wrong. I do not know...the United States, since it is the leader of the free world...must take gambles. We shall lose some; we shall win some...the public...expects us to win every gamble that we take. I do not expect that...[68]

In sum, the contention that Saigon was justified in preventing the unification elections is denied by overwhelming legal and factual evidence. What is true is that based on the reasonable supposition that these elections would produce favorable results, the Viet Minh laid down their arms and agreed to the strictly temporary division of the country. It is generally acknowledged that Hanoi eschewed violence south of the 17th parallel in the months following June 1954, if for no other reason than to maintain electoral support. In fact, in a 1961 White Paper, the State Department reproached the north for their "calculation" to win the elections and for focusing "during the post-Geneva period...on *political action*"; and applauded the south for refusing "to fall into this *well-laid trap*...," which "refusal came as a sharp disappointment to Hanoi."[69]

The refusal of South Vietnam, with United States backing, to hold the elections for unification, violated the provisions of the Geneva Accords that had made them acceptable to the Viet Minh. The fact that eventually the Vietnam conflict inevitably resumed its violent character is therefore not surprising. As Professors George Kahin and John Lewis have asked:

> When a military struggle for power ends on the agreed condition that the competition will be transferred to the political level, can the side which violates the agreed conditions legitimately expect that the military struggle will not be resumed?[70]

The State Department Memorandum itself provides the answer to Professors Kahin and Lewis' question.[71] It declares, with much supporting evidence, that it is an

> international law principle that a material breach of an agreement by one party entitles the other party at least to withhold compliance with an equivalent, corresponding or related provision until the defaulting party is prepared to honor its obligation.

B. The United States military build-up of South Vietnam was not justified.

As stated before, apart from the promise of unification by July 1956, the most essential aspect of the Geneva Accords was to prevent foreign military build-ups in Vietnam, and to this extent to *demilitarize* and *neutralize* the country. In order to render impossible any resumption of major hostilities, the military potential (armaments and personnel) of the French forces was to be frozen as of July 21, 1954, until their final withdrawal from the country. To achieve this purpose, the Cease-Fire Agreement contains extraordinarily careful and detailed provisions to guarantee the "Ban on the Introduction of [Foreign] Fresh Troops, Military Personnel, Arms and Ammunition, Military Bases"; and establishes elaborate machinery, including especially the International Commission for Supervision and Control in Vietnam, which was composed of India (as Chairman), Canada and Poland, with "fixed and mobile inspection teams" (Articles 34-35). "The introduction into Vietnam of any troop reinforcements and additional military personnel is prohibited" (Article 16), as is "the introduction into Vietnam of any reinforcements in the form of all types of arms, munitions and other war material, such as combat aircraft, naval craft, pieces of ordinance, jet engines and jet weapons, and armored vehicles" (Article 17, "Ban on Fresh Armaments and Munitions"). "The establishment of new military bases is prohibited throughout Vietnam territory" (Article 18). "No military base under the control of a foreign State may be established in [either] re-grouping zone" and the zones shall not "adhere to any military alliance and...not be used for the resumption of hostilities or to further an aggressive policy." (Article 19)

The replacement of "war material, arms and munitions" is also prohibited except under the most stringent provisions, including the prior and specific authorization of the ICC, "on the basis of piece-to-piece of the same type or of similar characteristics" as those physically present as of July 20, 1954, but "destroyed, damaged, worn out or used" hereafter. Obsolescence is pointedly omitted as a justification for replacement. There was to be no modernization, neither a quantitative nor qualitative build-up was permissible whether for military or for "police" purposes.

As to foreign (referring to the French) military personnel, only rotation on a "man-to-man basis" is permitted.[72]

1. The contention is incorrect that the United States military build-up in South Vietnam was until late 1961 within the limits permitted by the Geneva Accords.

It is common knowledge that ever since 1954 the United States engaged in a systematic and ever-increasing modernization and military build-up in South Vietnam. The State Department Memorandum admits that "prior to late 1961, South Vietnam has received *considerable* military equipment and supplies" from the United States (Sec. III, B), but asserts that "these actions were reported to the ICC and were justified as replacements for equipment in Vietnam in 1954..."

However, the Reports of the ICC are filled with statements about the clandestine character of those operations and describe some of the subterfuges used. For example, the Fifth, Sixth and Seventh ICC Reports (for periods August-December 1955; December 1955-July 1956; August 1956-April 1957, respectively) complain about the following devices introduced in violation of the Accords:

a) failure to request previous ICC authorization for introduction of "replacements" of foreign personnel or war materials; "facing the Commission with a *fait accompli*," to which "the Commission takes exception," by introducing 290 United States Army service corps personnel called TERM (Temporary Equipment Recovery Mission) before the ICC had acted on the application;

b) failure to submit manifests and other documents to the ICC;

c) failure to furnish advance notification to the ICC (for example, regarding United States Navy planes that "were visiting Saigon airport regularly") (Fifth Report, paragraph 28);

d) failure to reply to ICC inquiries, for example, with regard to the establishment of two new United States military missions—TRIM (Training Reorganization Inspection Mission) in March 1955, and CATO (Combat Arms Training Organization) in May 1956 (Seventh Report, paragraph 56);

e) claims "in many instances" that incoming war materials and military personnel were "in transit"; but failure to notify the ICC "about their exit, if any" (Seventh Report, paragraph 62);

f) preventing the ICC from physical access to incoming United States military planes and their cargo, by having them taxi directly to the military part of the Saigon airport, from which, contrary to the Accords, the ICC teams were excluded (Sixth Report, paragraph 63; Seventh Report, paragraphs 54, 63); or by claiming that certain United States "military and other planes" are "United States Embassy planes" (Seventh Report, paragraph 52); or by preventing the ICC's "prescribed control of Nha Be Harbour, near Saigon, since the end of August 1956" (paragraph 57); or preventing the ICC's reconnaissance of eight areas where, contrary to the Accords, new military airfields were allegedly being constructed (Seventh Report).[73]

In addition to specific instances, the Seventh Report states that ICC teams

> in South Vietnam were, as a rule, not able to go out on control duties, as the Government of the Republic of Vietnam did not cooperate. (paragraph 62; also paragraph 53)

and that, since August 1956, the South Vietnam regime no longer asked the ICC to authorize importation of war materials:

> the said Government did not ask for the Commission's approval, as required...in any case concerning [importation of] war materials. (paragraph 63)

In short, the ICC Reports show that the Diem regime and the United States contravened the military clauses of the Geneva Accords long before 1961. The use of devices such as those objected to in the ICC Reports indicates that the United States was aware of the illegality of its policy,[74] and undermines the contention of the State Department that, at least until late 1961, its policy was in accordance with the Geneva Accords.

2. The contention is incorrect that the United States military build-up since late 1961—admittedly contrary to the Geneva Accords—was legally justified.

The Memorandum states that, "As the Communist aggression intensified during 1961—the United States found it necessary in late 1961 to increase substantially the numbers of our military personnel and types of equipment introduced by this country into South Vietnam" (Sec. III, C) beyond the limits set by the Accords. However, it neglects to mention that the ICC—in fact, the Commission's Indian-Canadian majority—formally declared this and other aspects of United States military presence in South Vietnam to be in violation of the Geneva Accords.

South Vietnam did, indeed, advise the ICC on December 9, 1961, that, under the "right of 'self-defense'" it "found itself constrained...[to make a] request for increased aid..." Thereupon, a lengthy Special Report by the Indian-Canadian majority of the ICC:

a) specifically rejected the claim that this "increased aid" was permissible for South Vietnamese "self-defense," referring to "the *Geneva Agreement...and the obligations resulting therefrom*";

b) protested, as illegal, the fact that "Since December 1961, the Commission's Teams in South Vietnam have been *persistently denied the right to control and inspect...*";

c) stated that, nevertheless, the Teams "were able to observe the steady and continuous arrival of war material, including aircraft carriers with helicopters";

d) recites the introduction of large amounts of other United States war material and large numbers of United States military personnel (allegedly 5,000, soon to be increased to 8,000) into South Vietnam; and

e) culminates with the statement:

> ...the Commission concludes that the Republic of Vietnam has violated Articles 16 and 17 of the Geneva Agreement in receiving the increased military aid...[and] that, though there may not be any formal military alliance between the...United States of America and the Republic of Vietnam, the establishment of a U.S. Military Assistance Advisory Command in South Vietnam, as well as the introduction of a large number of U.S. military personnel...amounts to a factual military alliance, which is prohibited under Art. 19 of the Geneva Agreement.[75]

The failure of the State Department Memorandum to mention these fundamentally important findings in the ICC Report amounts to a startling distortion, especially because the Memorandum does quote other passages from the same Report—namely, those referring to northern support in violation of the Accords for the insurrection of the south (Sec. I, A). The Memorandum quotes those passages as its only specific evidence that "South Vietnam is being subjected to *armed attack* by Communist North Vietnam," although a little later (Sec. I, A), it states itself that such armed attack did not start until *three years later*, around February 1965 (just before the start of United States overt combat activities in the south and north).

By withholding from the reader the much more serious ICC findings about the illegality of the United States increased military build-up and of the United States-South Vietnamese *de facto* military alliance, the Memorandum conveys an impression in complete contradiction to the findings of the ICC Report,[76] which shows what the State Department conceals, namely, that the North's assistance to the insurgency in the south did not justify the earlier violations of the Accords, of a graver and more pervasive character, by South Vietnam and the United States.

C. United States participation in war actions started prior to the alleged "armed attack" occurring "before February 1965."

It must be emphasized that until February 1965, as is also stated in the Memorandum, the United States claimed to be justified in increasing the war potential of South Vietnam in a manner altogether inconceivable under the Accords: but it was not until February 1965 that the United States claimed a basis for *war* actions in South or North Vietnam. Furthermore, on February 7, 1965, when the United States did start its own direct war actions, it justified this as a *reprisal* for the Pleiku incidents (see Chap. V of this Analysis) and *not* as "collective self-defense" against an "armed attack" by North Vietnam on South Vietnam. The State Department Memorandum of March 4, 1966 is so far the most elaborate presentation of the official United States legal position regarding Vietnam. Yet, this document does not even mention the Pleiku incidents but alleges the occurrence of an indirect "armed attack" at some unspecified moment "before February 1965." By its own reasoning, then, the United States was not justified to wage war in "collective self-defense" prior to that "armed attack."

However, it has been public knowledge that long before February 1965, the United States played an active, and indeed, decisive part in the ever-worsening conflict, and that the conflict could otherwise never have attained such severe proportions. For example, bombing raids were routinely carried out long before February 1965, with planes supplied and equipped by the United States and were flown by crews composed of United States-trained Vietnamese and United States advisors. To cite two random illustrations: on March 29, 1962, the *New York Times* reported "the first comprehensive plan to pacify South Vietnam...*directly subsidized with United States money, military planning and technical aid*," the systematic burning down of villages;[77] and on March 28, 1965, the same paper reported, "*Defoliation operations have been carried out in South Vietnam since 1961*" with "*U.S. military forces...participating in most of the defoliation efforts*."[78]

If such actions could be justified at any time, they could not be justified between 1961 and early 1965, as the State Department itself claimed no right of collective self-defense prior to the "armed attack" that it alleges occurred around February 1965. These military actions taken by the United States since 1961 are also highly pertinent to the essential questions of the cause-and-effect relationship between United States and North Vietnamese involvement in the South Vietnam conflict.

V

The United States Started Its War Actions against North Vietnam as "Reprisal." This Reprisal Was Unlawful.

Until now, the most far-reaching escalation by the United States occurred on February 7, 1965, when military participation in the form of "advice" was changed to active United States war actions in South Vietnam, and when United States war actions were extended to North Vietnam.

These steps were so extraordinary, and so stunned the American people and the rest of the world, that the justification given for them is of particular significance. Especially noteworthy is the fact widely overlooked, even by the State Department Memorandum, that the United States did not attempt to justify these war actions as collective self-defense, or by reference to the United Nations Charter, SEATO, the Geneva Accords, or any other compact or commitment. Instead, the extension of the war into North Vietnam was officially explained as a *reprisal*; the active combat involvement in the south was not specifically explained but tacitly included in the theory of reprisal. Such a reprisal was unlawful.

Background and Announcement of "Reprisal." Early in February 1965, Soviet Premier Aleksei N. Kosygin visited Hanoi, while Mr.

McGeorge Bundy visited Saigon. A long dispatch by Seymour Topping from Saigon appeared in the *New York Times* on February 4th with the headline "*The Reds and Vietnam. Apparent Readiness to Ask Settlement.*" These reports aroused widespread speculation about whether the Soviet Union "would become an agent for arranging a negotiated settlement of the war in South Vietnam...the Soviet Union [being] apparently fearful that a continuation of the war in South Vietnam may lead to United States bombing of North Vietnam and its own involvement."[79]

On February 7, the *New York Times* published another dispatch by Mr. Topping, reporting that for four days, Mr. Bundy had discussed bombing of North Vietnamese targets.

Around 2 A.M. on February 7, "about 2 hours after the end of a 7-day cease-fire they had declared for the Lunar New Year celebration," the Vietcong made "two swift attacks on major [South] *Vietnamese* Army installations...The guerrillas, apparently using rifle grenades and 57 recoilless rifles, fired for 15 minutes into the headquarters of the [South Vietnamese] Army II corps area near Pleiku" and "the guerrillas' mortar crews fired on Camp Hollaway, a big airbase about 1 mile away."[80] Secretary of Defense Robert S. McNamara stated on television on February 7 that the American casualties were 7 killed and 109 wounded, and that "5 United States helicopters were destroyed, 9 to 11 damaged, and 6 United States fixed-wing aircraft were damaged." As to the adversary's fire-power, Mr. McNamara stated that "containers for 61 mortar rounds for 81 mm" were found outside the United States airstrip of Camp Hollaway.[81]

The United States Government termed these Vietcong actions around Pleiku in the early morning of February 7, 1965 as provocations. A White House statement issued the same day formally announced that

> *retaliatory* [air] attacks against barracks and staging areas...in *North Vietnam* [were] today [launched] *in response* to [these] provocations ordered and directed by the Hanoi regime.[82]

A. Reprisals involving the use of force are illegal.

Reprisals are actions which are in themselves unlawful, but which become lawful because they are taken in response to an unlawful act by the other side. While it is normally forbidden to injure others, reprisals are designed precisely to injure, as a response to an injury suffered.

Before the Covenant of the League of Nations and the Charter of the United Nations, such extraordinary self-help could consist of various injurious actions of various degrees of violence—for example, shelling a port, bombing a village, and the like. However, violent reprisals have been for a long time regarded with skepticism as they have so frequently involved the imposition of the will of powerful states upon weak states.[83] International law increasingly restricted the right of reprisal even before World War I.

In the present system of world order, injured states may take actions *short of violence*, but a general consensus prohibits the use of force in reprisal, in view of the categorical provisions of the United Nations Charter:

> With the adoption of the Charter of the United Nations forcible procedure [even] by methods falling short of war came under the general condemnation of the use of force, as prohibited by Article 2(3,4) of the Charter and, by implication, by Articles 39-40.[84]

As a study issued under the auspices of the Royal Institute of International Affairs (London) expresses it:

> It is now generally considered that reprisals involving the use or threat of force are illegal.[85]

The doctrine has also been consistently upheld by the United Nations Security Council. Various Council resolutions concurred in or even sponsored by the United States, have declared retaliation by armed force illegal and incompatible with the Purposes and Principles of the United Nations. Some of these resolutions are particularly pertinent to the Vietnam situation because they are inconsistent with any claim of a right of armed reprisal against violations of an armistice.[86]

In April 1964, in reference to British raids against Yemen in reprisal to Yemen attacks on the British Protectorate of Aden, the

Security Council condemned "reprisals as incompatible with the purposes and principles of the United Nations." In the preceding debate, Ambassador Adlai Stevenson emphasized United States disapproval of "retaliatory raids, wherever they occur and by whomever they are committed."[87]

The doctrine that no nation may, for purposes of "self-protection," use any military measure even if the measure would *not* endanger any lives, property or territory, was unanimously upheld in one of the most important and most often quoted judgments of the International Court of Justice, the *Corfu Channel Case* (1949). One issue in the case was whether the United Kingdom was justified in carrying out a mine-sweeping operation in Albanian territorial waters after mines actually exploding there had caused the death of 47 British seamen and considerable damage to two British destroyers. Evidently, the mine-sweeping operation could not have damaged, and was not claimed to have damaged, any Albanian lives, property or territory. Yet, although the World Court found that the mines had been emplaced illegally by Albania, it declared vigorously its view that subsequent mine-sweeping operations were illegal:

> ...The Court can only regard the alleged right of intervention as...a policy of force, such as has, in the past, given rise to most serious abuses and such as cannot, whatever may be the present defects in international organization, find a place in international law. Intervention is perhaps still less admissible in the particular form it would take here; for, from the nature of things, it would be reserved for the most powerful states, and might easily lead to perverting the administration of international justice itself.[88]

B. The United States claim to act in reprisal failed to satisfy the conditions under which reprisals would be permitted, even reprisals not involving any use of force.

Assuming, *arguendo*, that reprisals by violence were permitted, they would still constitute, by definition, acts that are in themselves unlawful, and that become permissible only if four absolute conditions are satisfied: a) the state intending to take reprisals must have suffered a legal wrong; b) before resorting to a reprisal, the injured state must have unsuccessfully endeavored to obtain redress; c) the reprisal must be directed against the guilty state; and d) the reprisal must be proportionate to the wrong suffered. The United States reprisals against North Vietnam violated each of these four conditions.

To begin with, no explanation was offered why the guerrilla attack at Pleiku on February 7, 1965 constituted a "provocation," or in what manner it differed, in law or fact, from previous skirmishes in South Vietnam. "Deliberate surprise" is a normal aspect of hostilities, and the United States had for years prior to that incident, planned and otherwise participated in "deliberate surprise attacks" on a much larger scale against the guerrillas. It is, therefore, not possible that the United States had suffered a legal wrong by the attack at Pleiku (condition a).[89]

Furthermore, as regards condition (c), the American reprisals were not directed against the insurgent forces in South Vietnam which staged the attack on Pleiku but against North Vietnam. To bomb a non-belligerent is an act of such gravity, and so abhorred by international law, that overwhelming evidence would be required to justify it. But on the crucial point—namely, whether the tort allegedly suffered by the United States can be imputed to North Vietnam—the statement by the United States merely asserts that the "provocations [were] ordered and directed by the Hanoi regime" and that "these attacks were only made possible by the continuing infiltration of personnel and equipment from North Vietnam." No proof was offered, and could hardly have been assembled during the few hours between the incidents and the alleged reprisals.

But even disregarding these two essential points, the two other conditions if a reprisal is to be lawful—previous effort at redress, and proportionality between the wrong committed as reprisal and the wrong suffered—were not fulfilled.

The duty to refrain from reprisals until efforts at redress have proven unsuccessful (condition b) has never been acknowledged in this instance as relevant by the United States. No reason was given for starting the massive bombing raids within a few hours after the relatively minor Pleiku incidents—a haste which, as has been mentioned, made impossible not only the collection of evidence, but also any effort at alternative means of redress.[90]

C. United States war actions violate, in particular, the requirement of proportionality.

Of the four absolute principles governing the right of even non-violent reprisal, perhaps the most important is the principle of proportionality. Under international law as well as under domestic law, any action that is in itself unlawful can at the most become lawful to the extent to which it is proportionate to the preceding illegality attributable to the other side. If, for example, the landlord fails in his obligation to provide heating, the tenant may (if the law permits) withhold part of the rent, but he may not burn down the house or kill the landlord.

In the *Naulilaa Case* (1928) between Portugal and Germany, which was the leading case about the law of reprisal before the United Nations Charter changed that law, the Mixed Tribunal stated:

> Reprisals are acts of self-help of the injured State…for unredressed acts contrary to international law on the part of the offending State. [Hence] the observance [by the injured State] of this or that rule of international law is temporarily suspended. [Reprisals] are limited by considerations of humanity and the rule of good faith.
>
> One should certainly consider as excessive, and therefore illegal, reprisals out of all proportion with the act which motivated them.[91]

The United States statement of February 7, 1965 shows an awareness of the rule of proportionality: it described the raids against North Vietnam as designed "to meet *these* attacks [at Pleiku]…the response is appropriate and fitting." However, the raids were actually the initiation of a new phase in the war in Vietnam that involved daily bombings of North Vietnam. These air attacks have from the outset vastly exceeded in destructiveness the Pleiku incidents, and have escalated into a massive, ever-growing war against North Vietnam.[92]

Can it be argued, however, that these United States military actions against the north are, contrary to Washington's statement, justifiable as reprisals for the support extended by Hanoi to the insurgency in the south? Such an argument would be untenable because, as has not been denied, the scope of United States assistance to Saigon—especially the military build-up in South Vietnam—has vastly exceeded Hanoi's assistance to the insurgents.[93] This disproportionate involvement exhausted and surpassed any claim by the United States to be entitled to further violent action as part of an overall right to make a proportionate response. Hence, the United States had not available, under any definition of reprisal, any further right of reprisal.

It should be added that justification of even the first United States raids against North Vietnam as a "reprisal" was rejected by the ICC.[94] *A fortiori*, subsequent air raids are even less susceptible to justification as reprisals.

VI

Even if the United States Were Lawfully Participating in the Collective Self-Defense of South Vietnam, Certain of Its Methods of Warfare Would Nevertheless Be Unlawful.

The fact that the United States characterized the beginning of the war against the north as "reprisal" damages the credibility of the present claim of "collective self-defense." If rights of collective self-defense did exist, the rule of proportionality would still apply. The only difference between self-defense and other forms of reprisal is that self-defense is a response to a particularly grave violation, namely, to an armed attack; and in such case the reprisal may consist of force.[95] But actions in self-defense

> must not be unreasonable or excessive, since the acts justified by the necessity of self-defense must be limited to that necessity and kept within it.[96]

This thoroughly established rule of proportionality was emphasized, for example, by the special Committee appointed by the League of Nations to investigate Japan's invasion of China. After a careful examination of the facts and conflicting statements, the Committee's Report concluded:

> ...the military operations carried out by Japan against China by land, sea and air are *out of all proportion* to the incident that occasioned the conflict [and]...can be justified neither on the basis of existing legal instruments nor on that of the right of self-defense.[97]

A decade earlier, the renowned Belgian jurist de Brouckere who was rapporteur of a League of Nations committee of legal experts stated:

> legitimate defense implies the adoption of measures *proportionate to the seriousness of the attack* and justified by the imminence of the danger.[98]

"Collective self-defense" does not therefore confer the right to bring systematic destruction upon a whole people by land, air and sea, including the widespread use of napalm and chemical bombs, crop destruction and assaults upon non-military targets. In Vietnam, the United States is conducting warfare with an intensity and ruthlessness that vastly exceeds permissible response (whether considered as a "reprisal" or as "collective self-defense") to any hostile actions cited in the State Department Memorandum, even assuming *contrary to fact* that the other side was guilty of an illegal provocation.

The appalling extent of destruction being wrought upon South and North Vietnam was partly disclosed by the testimony of Secretary of Defense Robert S. McNamara:

> There are 61,000 tons of bombs in inventory in Southeast Asia, Mr. McNamara began. The 50,000 tons of bombs dropped in March [1966] compared with an average of 48,000 tons a month dropped over Europe and Africa in World War II and an average of 17,500 tons a month dropped during the 37 months of the Korean War.
>
> Last December [he said] United States plans for 1966 allowed for a total of 638,000 tons of bombs to be dropped in Vietnam. This would be about 91% of the total dropped in Korea in 37 months, and 37% of the total dropped from June, 1942, to May, 1945 in Africa and Europe during World War II.[99]

It must be noted that this recital refers only to bombs, and omits all other types of weapons used.

Field Manual No. 27-10 of the United States Army declares in its section titled *"Basic Rules and Principles"*:

2. *Purposes of the Law of War*

The conduct of armed hostilities on land is regulated by the law of land warfare...It is inspired by the desire to diminish the evils of war by

a) Protecting both the combatants and noncombatants from unnecessary suffering;

b) Safeguarding certain fundamental human rights of persons who fall into the hands of the enemy, particularly prisoners of war, the wounded and sick, and civilians; and

c) Facilitating the restoration of peace.

3. *Basic Principles*

a) Prohibitive Effect. The law of war places limits on the exercise of a belligerent's power in the interests mentioned in paragraph 2 and requires that belligerents refrain from employing any kind or degree of violence which is not actually necessary for military purposes and that they conduct hostilities with regard to the principles of humanity and chivalry.

...Military necessity has been generally rejected as a defense, [that is, as a permission] for acts forbidden by the customary and conventional laws of war...

b) Binding on States and Individuals. The law of war is binding not only upon States as such but upon individuals and, in particular, the members of their armed forces.[100]

A further relevant provision of the Field Manual:

7. These Treaty provisions are in large part but formal and specific applications of general principles of the unwritten law. While solemnly obligatory only as between the parties thereto, they may be said also to represent modern international public opinion as to how belligerents and neutrals should conduct themselves...

For these reasons, the treaty provisions quoted herein will be strictly observed and enforced by U.S. forces...[101]

The State Department makes the very important, although self-evident statement that the international law of war *applies* in the Vietnam conflict.[102] It may suffice here to quote some of the basic Regulations of the Hague Convention IV of 1907, which have not only been for decades part of the "supreme law of the land," but have long since been recognized by nations, including the United States, as expressing "the practice of civilized nations at war":

Section I. Chapter II. *Prisoners of War*

> *Article 4.* Prisoners of war...must be humanely treated...
>
> *Article 7.* The Government into whose hands prisoners of war have fallen is charged with their maintenance.
>
> In the absence of a special agreement between the belligerents, prisoners of war shall be treated as regards board, lodging, and clothing on the same footing as the troops of the Government who [sic] captured them.

Section II. Chapter I. *Means of Injuring the Enemy, Sieges and Bombardments.*

> *Article 22.* The right of belligerents to adopt means of injuring the enemy is not unlimited.
>
> *Article 23.* ...it is especially forbidden—
>
> a) to employ poison or poisoned weapons;
>
> b) to kill or wound treacherously individuals belonging to the hostile nation or army;
>
> c) to kill or wound an enemy who, having laid down his arms, or having no longer means of defense, has surrendered at discretion;
>
> • • •
>
> e) to employ arms, projectiles, or material calculated to cause unnecessary suffering;
>
> • • •
>
> g) to destroy or seize the enemy's property, unless such destruction or seizure be imperatively demanded by the necessities of war; [general prohibition of "wanton destruction" of any enemy property, whether it be an electric power plant, or a bag of rice, and whether by military means or otherwise.]

Article 25. The attack or bombardment, by whatever means, of towns, villages, dwellings or buildings which are undefended is prohibited.

Article 27. In sieges and bombardments all necessary steps must be taken to spare, as far as possible, buildings dedicated to religion, art, science or charitable purposes, historic monuments, hospitals, and places where the sick and wounded are collected, provided they are not being used at the time for military purposes.[103]

Numerous reports and photographs published in the American and world press indicate violations of international rules of warfare regarding, for example, the treatment of prisoners of war, the treatment of civilians, and the limits of destruction of enemy property.[104] The United States Army Field Manual mentioned above, unequivocally asserts the validity of those international Conventions (treaties) to which the United States is a party:

7. (b) *Force of Treaties under the Constitution.* Under the Constitution of the United States, treaties constitute part of the "supreme law of the land"...In consequence, *treaties relating to the law of war* have a force equal to that of laws enacted by Congress. Their provisions *must be observed with the same strict regard for both the letter and the spirit of the law* which is required with respect to the *Constitution* and statutes enacted in pursuance thereof.[105]

These statements make it abundantly clear that any violations by the United States of the law of warfare in South or North Vietnam constitute violations of United States domestic law as well as international law.

VII

Foreign Military Intervention in a Civil War Is Illegal under International Law.

A. The conflict in South Vietnam is a civil war (apart from United States intervention).

1. The position of the United States is based entirely on the contention that the warfare in South Vietnam is not a civil war, but consists of resistance against external aggression ("armed attack from the north"). Support for the insurgents by their northern fellow-countrymen in the face of ever more massive United States intervention has been clearly given, but this does not alter the essential character of the conflict as a civil war. To contend that the conflict in Vietnam is not a civil war contradicts the factual circumstances of the South Vietnamese tragedy ever since 1954. Among other things, such a view overlooks, and thus discounts, the numerous repressive measures taken over many years by Diem and his successor regimes (usually in consultation with United States advisors) to subdue the formidable indigenous opposition. It also fails to explain how outside agents could compel millions of South Vietnamese to make the sacrifices they

have been making for so long—what Senator Claiborne Pell has called their "fervor."[106] This rebellion in South Vietnam is against a regime which many domestic groups consider foreign-imposed and foreign-dominated and which endeavors, by war actions, to gain control over the society. The insurgency by the Vietcong and their non-combatant supporters is only the most overt form of domestic opposition against the Saigon regime. The opposition of other elements in South Vietnamese society leads even to a variety of antigovernment demonstrations, itself a rare phenomenon during wartime. As Senator Wayne Morse pointed out, "it was often said in the [1966 Senate] hearings [by adherents of the United States policy] that a defense of coastal areas—or enclaves—would cause the collapse of the Saigon government...We cannot even restrain the use of U.S. forces to certain areas without its collapsing."[107]

2. As mentioned above, the State Department Memorandum itself implies that before 1964 the so-called "infiltration" consisted largely of South Vietnamese returning to their homeland. Even if they were returning in order to participate in the fighting as guerrillas, this would not change the character of the conflict from a civil war.

The Declaration of Honolulu also implicitly conceded that the conflict had its origin in the internal situation in South Vietnam and not in an external armed attack. The stress which the Declaration placed upon the urgent need for basic social reform can be read as an acknowledgment that the war is essentially a revolt against domestic conditions. To this may be added the existence among civilian groups of a desperate desire for peace and for independence from foreign intervention observed and commented upon by all neutral reporters.[108]

3. When, early in 1966, the Senate Foreign Relations Committee held its first Hearings on Vietnam,[109] the question of whether the conflict should be regarded as a civil war was one of the main issues. For example, Senator Pell observed:

> This question of whether it is a Vietnamese war or an American war...concerns us here...the more you read about it, the more you realize it is really one country, one people, one basic language...so we have to determine how much of this is a civil war...[110]

Senator Frank Church, drawing some analogies to the United States Civil War, said:

> Now, you can look at the war in Vietnam as a covert invasion of the south by the north, or...as some scholars do, as basically an indigenous war to which the north has given a growing measure of aid and abetment, but either way it is a war between Vietnamese to determine what the ultimate kind of government is going to be for Vietnam...
>
> When I went to school, that was a civil war. I am told these days it is not a civil war any more.[111]

Former Ambassador George F. Kennan stated:

> ...the word "aggression" with regard to what we are facing today in Vietnam is confusing...the border between North and South Vietnam...was not meant...to be a border between states...This is, of course, in part the invasion of one country, if one wants to describe it that way, by forces of another country, although all of these things involve stretching of terms. But in any case, it is not just that. It is also a civil conflict within South Vietnam and one of great seriousness...[112]

Senator George G. Aiken pointed out:

> according to the Department of Defense Statistics, there have been a total of 63,000 infiltrators from North Vietnam since 1960, and during that period...we have killed 112,000 Vietcong.[113]

When he asked Secretary of State Dean Rusk whether these and other United States statistics "indicate that there are civil war aspects to this struggle," Mr. Rusk replied:

> There are elements of civil war in this situation, but the heart of the problem of peace is the external aggression.[114]

At the final session of the Hearings, the Chairman of the Committee, Senator J. W. Fulbright, declared:

> ...this war...goes back to the time when indigenous Vietnamese nationalists...most unfortunately, from our point of view, were led by Communists...These nationalistic Communists were twice betrayed, once by the French in 1946 after they thought they had made an agreement for independence, and later in 1956 by President Diem who, with the support of the Americans, refused to hold unification

> elections. After 1956, the struggle became a *civil war* between the Diem government and the Vietcong...
>
> After all, Vietnam is their country. It is not our country...We have no historical right. We are obviously intruders from their point of view. We represent the old Western imperialism in their eyes... Other countries have had civil wars; we had one...You can remember the feelings...[115]

B. International law prohibits outside intervention in civil war.

1. The overwhelming evidence shows that the Saigon "Government" is being opposed militarily by the Vietcong and by other groups in South Vietnam using non-military means. This conclusion has great political significance but it is also of great legal significance. The legal situation is admittedly complex; or, more correctly, the refusal to hold the unification elections has resulted in complex problems of international law regarding the status of a regime in a temporary zone that wishes at any price to be maintained as the government of an independent country.

Whenever an unusual situation theoretically permits different interpretations, it is considered good legal craftsmanship to be guided by the interpretation that is least contrived and least likely to lead to consequences destructive of the basic principles of the legal order.[116]

By insisting that the situation in Vietnam is not a civil war, the State Department seems fully conscious of the dangerous implications of asserting that the United States is entitled under international law to intervene in a civil war. Evidently, if such right were to exist for one intervener, it would exist correspondingly for any intervener on the other side. North Vietnam's much smaller amount of aid to the southern insurgents would then be equally justified, and could not constitute indirect aggression, much less "armed attack." The entire justification for United States intervention would collapse. Furthermore, adherence to such a doctrine could cause dire results in the future. For a doctrine sponsored by the United States that would permit outside states at the request of a warring faction—or even only on the side of the legitimate government—to intervene in civil war as substantially as has the United States, would create a legal precedent available to other states in future civil wars—for example, to the Soviet Union and Communist China. These states have had the right to bomb American territory by the same reasoning used by the United States to vindicate bombing North Vietnam.

However, the denial of the civil war character of the Vietnam conflict does not achieve the State Department's purpose of justifying only United States intervention, while closing the door to analogous interventions by other powers. The State Department's doctrine—that North Vietnam's involvement in the south constitutes "armed attack"—would still permit any country in the future to bomb and defoliate any other country intervening in a civil war by characterizing the latter's intervention as "armed attack." Hence, by its own construction, the State Department Memorandum conjures up arguments capable of leading to unpredictably ominous developments destructive of the world legal order.[117]

2. The contention that the conflict is not an example of civil strife but has arisen from an external aggression is also contradicted by the attitude of the United States toward the NLF in South Vietnam. The State Department Memorandum ignores the existence of the NLF. Yet the fact is that it does exist; it controls much of South Vietnam and in such areas provides the actual government. The conflict in South Vietnam is being fought between the Saigon government (assisted by the United States) and the NLF (assisted to a much smaller extent by North Vietnam) which wishes to overthrow the Saigon Government. In fact, all military operations by the United States against North Vietnam are constantly represented as an *adjunct*, as *incidental* to the war against the NLF, and undertaken to weaken northern assistance to the actual adversary, the NLF forces.

3. If the conflict is a civil war, then United States unilateral intervention contravenes not only the Geneva Accords but also the general undertaking, fundamental in international law, that one state has no right to intervene in the internal affairs of another.

The Charter of the United Nations confirms in Article 2(7) the principle of non-intervention by prohibiting even the United

Nations "to intervene in matters which are essentially within the domestic jurisdiction of any State." It has been generally assumed that this principle applies to civil wars, so that even the United Nations must not intervene in them in any way (unless a breach of the peace, threat to the peace, or act of aggression is involved; but this is, pursuant to Article 39 of the Charter, exclusively for the United Nations to decide). Certainly, if the United Nations is required to stay aloof from civil strife, individual states have the same obligation. The logic of this duty (namely, to prevent military escalation through intervention, counterintervention, and mutual counterintervention between interveners) has been discussed above. In fact, the weight of opinion among international lawyers is to place great stress upon this duty of nonintervention.[118]

4. However, it must again be emphasized that this does not mean that other states must sit idly by if and when a civil war is being converted by any outside state from a *domestic* struggle for power into a threat to *international* peace through aggression. As has been shown, the Security Council (and, under the *Uniting for Peace Resolution*, the General Assembly) can then initiate appropriate action.

VIII

The SEATO Treaty of 1954 Does Not "Commit" the United States To Take Military Action in Vietnam.

The claims of the United States Memorandum that American military involvement in Vietnam fulfills a "commitment" arising out of its treaty obligations are so unfounded and so deceptively presented that they earned the severe condemnation of so strong a supporter of United States policy in Vietnam as Congressman Laird.[119]

It has been shown that no such commitment can be based upon the Geneva Accords, nor can the United States course find any legal vindication in the SEATO arrangements.

A. The claim of SEATO obligations is discredited by its belatedness.

As late as in March 1965 (after the United States had embarked on open war actions in Vietnam), the State Department Memorandum entitled "Legal Basis for United States Actions Against North Vietnam" did not mention SEATO; nor, significantly, did President

Johnson in his press conference on July 28, 1965 explaining "why we are in Vietnam." The SEATO argument is the latest of the justifications advanced by the State Department,* one that Arthur Schlesinger Jr. has characterized as an "intellectual disgrace."

Arthur Krock has described its origin as follows:

> [The President] utilized the provocation of the Tonkin Gulf attack on the Seventh Fleet by North Vietnamese gunboats to get a generalized expression of support from Congress. This worked well enough until it was argued, against public record, as approval by Congress of any expansion of the war the President might make in an unforeseeable future. Then Rusk shifted the major basis for the claim to the SEATO compact.[120]

B. In fact, United States military intervention in Vietnam violates the SEATO Treaty.

1. In the first place, at the outset (Article 1) the Treaty pledges the Parties to respect the Charter of the United Nations; furthermore, Article 6 specifically emphasizes that no Party may interpret SEATO "as affecting in any way" its obligations under the Charter.[121]

Hence, insofar as United States actions in Vietnam violate the Charter, their illegality is in no way rectified or diminished by the SEATO Treaty; on the contrary, such violations are automatically also in contravention to the SEATO Treaty.

2. Even if the SEATO Treaty did not reaffirm the obligations of SEATO Parties under the United Nations Charter, any action pursuant to SEATO which violated the Charter would still be unlawful; for, under Article 103 of the Charter—the supremacy clause—the United States has pledged to subordinate all other treaty obligations to the Charter:

> In the event of a conflict between the obligations of the Members of the United Nations under the present Charter and their obligations

* In November 1966 the Senate Foreign Relations Committee secured official clearance for the release of the transcript of the August 6, 1964 hearings on the Tonkin Bay Resolution, which disclosed that Secretary of State Rusk then testified: "We are not acting specifically under the SEATO Treaty."

> under any *other* international agreement, *their obligations under the Charter shall prevail.*

3. The SEATO Treaty also pledges the Parties to respect the Geneva Accords[122] which had been agreed upon only a few weeks earlier. The Treaty could hardly do otherwise; for a compact between A and B cannot alter or diminish their obligations under another compact, toward C. The SEATO Treaty, therefore, did not and could not, in law, impair the Geneva stipulations.

Hence, the "protective umbrella" that SEATO provided for "the free territory under the jurisdiction of the State of Vietnam"[123] (the Diem Regime) could legally be applicable only until the unification of Vietnam in July 1956, because thereafter such territory would become part of unified Vietnam. In fact, awareness of the validity of the Geneva Declaration is evidenced by the extraordinary device of providing for such an "umbrella" in the SEATO Treaty to protect an entity that was prohibited by the Geneva Accords from joining SEATO.

4. The State Department Memorandum misquotes the SEATO Treaty on essential points. It asserts that Article 4(1) SEATO creates an "obligation...to meet the common danger in the event of armed aggression." The term "armed aggression" is not to be found in the Treaty. Article 4(1) speaks of "aggression by means of armed attack," and as shown above, the Memorandum fails to establish that an "armed attack" has occurred.

Furthermore, in case of an "armed attack," the United States would merely have had the right, but not the obligation,[124] to assist the "free territory" of Vietnam. The nonexistence of an obligation is also shown by the impossibility of identifying to whom the United States was obligated. It was certainly not obligated to South Vietnam, for South Vietnam was not and could not be a Party to SEATO. The obligation, then, could be said to exist only in relation to the other SEATO Parties. This interpretation would produce an absurd situation, one in which United States military intervention would be viewed as satisfying an obligation toward, for example, France (which has publicly denounced the United States course); and, to take another random example, France and Great Britain would be violating an obligation toward Pakistan by refusing to intervene in Vietnam!

5. The State Department Memorandum also ignores the specific distinction which SEATO makes between "armed attack" on the one hand, and "subversive activities directed from outside" on the other hand. [125] Yet, no SEATO partner is entitled unilaterally to disregard this basic distinction between "armed attack" and "subversive activities," and unilaterally to "interpret" subversive activities as if the SEATO Treaty characterizes "subversive activities" as "armed attack."[126]

The SEATO Treaty stipulates explicitly in Article 4(2) that if a "territory [like Vietnam] is threatened in any way other than by armed attack [which, by the Treaty's whole construction, includes "subversion from outside"]...the [SEATO] Parties shall consult immediately in order to agree on the measures which should be taken for the common defense."

SEATO therefore *prohibits* unilateral military action. Indeed, it requires previous unanimous *agreement* by the other seven partners before any SEATO party could take any "measure," including a *non*-military measure, let alone combat assistance. In 1964, the United States interpreted the unanimity principle to mean that "measures" could be taken in the absence of a dissenting vote among the SEATO partners.

6. *The other SEATO Parties have not authorized United States war actions in Vietnam.* On May 24, 1966 Secretary of State Dean Rusk, referring to a SEATO meeting in April 1964, said:

> In April 1964, the SEATO Council of Ministers declared that the attack on the Republic of Vietnam was an "aggression...directed, supplied and supported by the Communist regime in North Vietnam in flagrant violation of the Geneva Accords of 1954 and 1962." They also declared that the defeat of the "Communist campaign is essential" and that the members of SEATO should remain prepared to take further steps in fulfillment of their obligations under the treaty. Only France did not join in these declarations.[127]

The Communique of that SEATO meeting, dated April 15, 1964, shows that the Ministers did *not* characterize the situation as "attack."[128] The all-important term, "attack"—which alone could have made Article 4(1) of the SEATO Treaty operative and thus have authorized United States combat action—was used by Mr. Rusk two years later. Furthermore, such combat involvement in Vietnam was still nine months away, and in April 1964 was not even claimed by the United States to be justified; and the SEATO Minister's Communique did not sanction any combat action by any SEATO Party. Indeed, Mr. Rusk's statement in May 1966 is careful not to make such claim.[129]

When the United States started its own combat actions in Vietnam, it did not convene the SEATO powers, perhaps because of the possibility of dissenting votes. Thus the United States can hardly claim that SEATO obligates it to its present course when in fact it evaded its treaty obligation to obtain collective permission for "Collective Defense"—even the name of the treaty implies collective decisions.[130]

7. Finally, the United States actions are in contravention of Article 53 of the United Nations Charter which (except in the case of self-defense against armed attack) unequivocally prohibits enforcement action under regional arrangements except with previous Security Council authorization:

> No enforcement action shall be taken under regional arrangements or by regional agencies without the authorization of the Security Council.[131]

Hence, even if the United States had obtained the required consent from its SEATO partners, the United States would furthermore require authorization from the United Nations Security Council to establish the legality of its "measures."

This provision of the Charter is of greatest importance, especially in the case of regional action by a permanent member of the Security Council. For, once such a state had taken regional enforcement action, it would thereafter possess the power of veto and could always prevent the Security Council from stopping or altering its "enforcement action." In any case, consonant with basic United Nations principles, the rule is that no Member state may take regional "enforcement action" unless authorized by the Security Council.[132] The United States has neither sought nor obtained such authorization for its actions in Vietnam. It also did not live up to Article 52(2) of the Charter, which obligates any Party to a regional arrangement to "make every effort to achieve pacific settlement of local disputes through such regional arrangements...before referring them to the Security Council."[133]

8. To summarize, United States actions in South and North Vietnam are in violation of the SEATO Treaty and of several Charter provisions incorporated into the SEATO Treaty because:

a) Under SEATO's definition of "armed attack," the situation in South Vietnam does not constitute "armed attack," so that United States unilateral measures in Vietnam are not permitted under SEATO, nor under Article 51 of the United Nations Charter.

b) Even if SEATO would obligate the United States to act in a manner contrary to the United Nations Charter (which it does not), such obligation would be overridden by the United States obligations under the Charter (Article 103).

c) The SEATO Treaty requires respect for the Geneva Accords of 1954 which provide for unification of Vietnam by July 1956; it is therefore highly questionable whether SEATO's unusual "protective umbrella" provisions for the "free territory" of South Vietnam continued to be operative after July 1956 when pursuant to the Geneva Accords (and, therefore, also pursuant to SEATO which incorporates the Geneva Accords) that "free territory" was to cease to exist as a separate entity.

d) The United States has failed to abide by the procedures for collective decision-making required by the SEATO agreement and has resorted to measures on a unilateral basis in Vietnam.

e) Even if the United States had obtained collective backing, regional enforcement is legal only in the event that it is authorized in advance by the Security Council of the United Nations.[134]

IX

The United States Has Not Fulfilled Its Obligations Toward the United Nations. The Security Council Has Not Tacitly Approved the Military Course of the United States in Vietnam.

As the State Department Memorandum affirms, the United States has on some occasions reported to the Security Council on "measures it has taken"—that is, *after* certain war measures had been taken. Such reports could only have two results: to embarrass the friends of the United States on the Council, who knew that to recommend a more constructive course would merely antagonize the United States; and to challenge its adversaries on the Council, who knew that any more far-reaching Council resolutions could always be vetoed by the United States.

At the end of January 1966, during a suspension of the United States raids against North Vietnam, the United States for the first time asked the Security Council for a discussion looking toward a peaceful settlement. But immediately after making this request in the United Nations and despite Senator Fulbright's warning on January 28 that "If we resume the bombing, then we are committed and will have passed the Rubicon,"[135] devastating bombing raids against the north were resumed. In the words of Senator Henry Aiken, these raids were called "new steps which may lead to a cataclysmic world conflict."[136] Furthermore, the United States virtually precluded any effective role for the Security Council by scheduling a dramatic war conference with Premier Ky at the same time as proposing peace talks in the United Nations. The ambiguity of United States action was accentuated by the tenor of the Honolulu Declaration publicized a few days later,[137] especially the implication of a harmony of goals existing between President Johnson and Premier Ky.

The State Department Memorandum contends that the United States "did not interfere with United Nations consideration of the conflict" and implies that, since the Security Council "has not seen fit to act," it has thereby tacitly approved the course of the American Government in Vietnam. This inference is scarcely credible.

Neither the United States nor any other Member would accept the legal proposition that non-action by the United Nations implied tacit approval; just as under domestic law, non-action by a domestic organ does not legalize an unlawful act. Such an implication is, furthermore, denied by the following facts:

1. First of all, most United Nations Member governments are gravely concerned about the Vietnam tragedy,[138] as public pronouncements inside and outside the United Nations have shown. Efforts at quiet diplomacy under the auspices of the United Nations have also received public attention, such as the attempts by Amintore Fanfani, the President of the 20th Session of the General Assembly and by Secretary General U Thant, supplemented by persevering appeals and constant warning against the futility of solving Vietnam's problems by military methods. By Spring 1966, U Thant stated that "the so-called 'fight for democracy' is no longer relevant to the realities of the situation," as "twenty years of outside intervention" are reducing the problem to sheer "national survival" of Vietnam.[139]

2. The assumption that silence indicates approval reverses the clear law and logic of the Charter. In the absence of an "armed attack," United States intervention could, from the start, have been justified only by a *previous* order or authorization from the competent United Nations organ. If throughout these years South Vietnam believed that there existed a "threat to the peace,

breach of the peace, or act of aggression," it had the right to ask the Security Council for appropriate action. The United States, of course, enjoyed the same right. In any case, it was under an obligation to refrain from intervention unless ordered or authorized to do so by the Security Council.

It is also of the highest legal and political importance that the Security Council is extremely flexible in the measures it may order or authorize; and that, as numerous precedents show (as illustrated by the Dutch-Indonesian, Arab-Israeli, Indian-Pakistani disputes) the Council prefers peaceful settlement even when, under the Charter, it could impose military sanctions.[140]

3. But could not the Security Council have been stalemated, for example, by a Soviet or French veto? Ever since the adoption of the *Uniting for Peace Resolution* in 1951, the United Nations General Assembly has possessed considerable powers if the Security Council is stalemated. In 1956 the *Uniting for Peace Resolution* was invoked by the General Assembly, after a stalemate in the Security Council, to permit United Nations action in the Suez crisis. The argument, then, that such stalemate, or even less its mere prospect, could justify unilateral action by a state was answered by Derek Bowett, one of the authorities relied on by the Memorandum:

> Since the Acheson Plan [*Uniting for Peace Resolution*] it is not possible to make the assumption that there is no competent organ of the United Nations really capable of authorizing collective action in the interests of international peace and security. This new development [it occurred in 1951] seems to take the force from the argument...for extending the concept of collective self-defense to cover intervention by any state to assist the victim of aggression.[141]

The General Assembly is free from the veto and possesses the residual right to characterize a situation as a "threat to the peace"; given this possibility, individual states make themselves "*highly suspect*" if they insist upon making such characterization on their own:

> for a state or group of states...to make such a characterization on their own initiative...would be highly suspect when two-thirds majority of world opinion cannot be secured in favor of such a course.[142]

4. The State Department's assertion, "At no time has the Security Council taken any action to restore peace and security in Southeast Asia," overlooks some relevant information: first of all, neither South Vietnam nor the United States ever brought a complaint about the alleged aggression by North Vietnam before the Security Council; and secondly, the United States *circumvented* Security Council action by its unilateral war actions. The statement also implies that the Council should have acted, and that, since it did not, the duty to restore peace and security falls to the United States. It must be noted that the State Department Memorandum does not refer here to resisting an armed attack, but invokes the broader language of Article 51 about "restoring peace and security"—throughout Southeast Asia.[143]

It is the essence of world order—and merely reconfirmed by the Charter of the United Nations—that no single State may assume the function of what is sometimes called the policeman of the world. Actually, a state claiming the right to bomb and destroy a foreign territory on its own discretionary determination that this is required "to restore peace and security," acts simultaneously as policeman, judge and executioner. This right to impose its own interpretation of "peace and security" on a global scale has never been conceded to any state by the international community. It is, for example, altogether incompatible with the Kellogg-Briand Pact of 1928, which outlawed war as an instrument of national policy. The permission, exceptionally granted in the Charter, to use force in self-defense against armed attack is precisely restricted to resisting an armed attack, and that grant is the outer limit of national discretion to use force.

It should be emphasized again at this point, that these are not mere legalisms. The distinctions made in the Charter and urged here, determine the life and death of many Americans, and many more Vietnamese. And if the doctrine proposed by the United States were to be followed by any principal state with which the United States disagreed, the outcome of the confrontation might well be global nuclear war.

5. *The Korean Precedent Indicates the Illegality, Not the Legality, of the United States Military Intervention in Vietnam.* The assumption of any tacit approval of United States action in Vietnam is strikingly refuted by the attempt of the State Department Memorandum to draw an analogy between Vietnam and

Korea. On this point, the Memorandum opens itself to such obvious refutation that its mention of Korea as an alleged precedent is difficult to understand. The Memorandum claims that the action of the United Nations regarding Korea, "clearly established the principle that there is no greater license for one zone of a temporarily divided state to attack the other zone than there is for one State to attack another State…South Vietnam has the same right to defend itself and to organize collective defense against an armed attack from the north"; it then quotes a Security Council Resolution of June 25, 1951 which characterized the armed attack from North Korea as a breach of the peace.

If these statements are disentangled, they should read as follows: In the Korean case, it was the Security Council, and neither the United States nor South Korea, which determined that there had been an armed attack that constituted a breach of the peace. South Korea did *not* organize collective self-defense, and therefore the question remained unanswered whether as a zone of a "temporary divided State" it *could* have done so legally, even in response to an armed attack. *If* in the Vietnam case the Security Council had also determined the occurrence of an armed attack or any other breach of the peace, and *if* in 1965 it had authorized military sanctions against North Vietnam as it did in 1950 regarding Korea, then United States involvement in such sanctions would have been legally justified.

The basic differences between Korea and Vietnam have been underscored by, among others, General Matthew Ridgeway. The State Department Memorandum does nothing to convince an observer that the Korean precedent establishes legality of the United States course in Vietnam. The United Nations action in Korea, instead of legitimating the United States actions in Vietnam, reveals their crucial deficiency by pointing up the difference between community authorization in Korea and unilateral action in Vietnam. It is pertinent to note that the United States did not justify its assistance to South Korea as collective self-defense but explained its role as one of rendering assistance to the United Nations by implementing the Security Council's Resolution of June 25, 1950, which determined (a) that an armed attack had occurred and (b) that that action constituted a breach of the peace.[144]

6. The United Nations Charter reflects the realities of power in the world: it is well-known that any permanent Member of the Security Council can, not only by the actual use of the veto, but by the implied threat or obvious expectation of its use, prevent action by the Security Council. Whether the veto will actually be used merely depends on the tactics of other Members. They may press for a Resolution, knowing that it will be vetoed, or, judging all the circumstances, prefer not to exacerbate further an already explosive situation by acrimonious debate which could not lead to a constructive solution. In view of the adamant position of the United States regarding Vietnam, members of the Security Council appear to have chosen this latter course. Rather than implying, therefore, that this amounts to tacit approval, it would seem more correct legally and factually to say that the Security Council has been inhibited by the United States course in Vietnam.

All in all, the question is not only whether the United States had submitted reports and introduced resolutions of a formalistic nature in the United Nations. The question is whether the United States has fulfilled its obligations toward its own people and toward the organized community of nations to use all avenues prescribed in the Charter to save this country from war.

X

The United States Failed To Seek a Peaceful Solution As Prescribed by the Charter of the United Nations.

The duty to seek peaceful settlement of international disputes was established, as mentioned above, in such treaties as the Kellogg-Briand Pact of 1928 and the Rio de Janeiro Treaty of 1933, and formed a principle of general international law long before the United Nations Charter.

Article 33(1) of the Charter confirmed this duty:

> The parties to any dispute, the continuance of which is likely to endanger the maintenance of international peace and security, shall first of all, seek a solution by negotiation, enquiry, mediation, conciliation, arbitration, judicial settlement, resort to regional agencies or arrangements, or other peaceful means of their own choice.[145]

The legally obligatory character of these provisions has been emphasized by Senator Ernest Gruening as follows:

> This Article does not say that disputing nations may do this but that they shall do it, and lists eight alternative methods, which should be used first of all. Now we may well ask, did we, the United States, when there were

> violations of the Geneva agreements, seek a solution by negotiation? We did not. Did we seek a solution by enquiry? We did not. Did we seek a solution by mediation? We did not. Did we seek a solution by conciliation? We did not. Did we seek a solution by arbitration? We did not. Did we seek a solution by judicial settlement? We did not. Did we seek a solution by resorting to regional agencies or arrangements? We did not. Or did we seek a solution by "other peaceful means of our [their] own choice"? We did not.[146]

Senator Vance Hartke, among others, has sharply criticized the apparent tendency of the United States to intensify its military policy whenever prospects for a negotiated settlement seem to improve.[147]

The State Department Memorandum refers at length to the developments over the years in South Vietnam and to United States involvement in them; yet it dismisses with a peremptory footnote what it itself calls the Charter's "peaceful settlement obligation." In that footnote, it merely relies upon "the obvious proposition that a victim of armed aggression is not required to sustain the attack undefended while efforts are made to find a political solution with the aggressor." (Memorandum, footnote 7.)

This trivial and irrelevant assertion is neither responsive to the documented history of the United States involvement in Vietnam, nor is it consistent with the clear wording of Article 33. Curiously, it overlooks the fact that ever since 1954, a decade before the alleged armed attack is said to have occurred, no efforts to find a political solution were made by South Vietnam or the United States. It also overlooks the continuing Charter duty to seek peaceful settlement during war.[148] The State Department position is also refuted by the peaceful settlement that was found for neighboring Laos, where similar developments threatened to undo the 1954 Geneva Accords.

The 1962 Settlement for Laos Is an Example of Peaceful Solution which Could Be Followed for Vietnam. "By the close of the year 1960 a full-scale civil war was being waged in Laos." Thereupon, "after months of intergovernmental negotiation," a conference of 14 governments, including the United States, labored at Geneva for more than one year until, in July 1962, it reached a statement by Laos accepting neutrality and a "responsive declaration by the other 13 Conference members."

"In its Statement, Laos resolved 'to build a peaceful, neutral, independent, democratic, unified and prosperous Laos' and undertakes a number of specific steps to implement that policy," for example, "'not to interfere in the internal affairs of other countries.'" not to "'allow any foreign interference in [its own] internal affairs'...not to enter into any military alliance or any agreement inconsistent with its neutrality, not to permit any foreign military base to be established on Laos territory, not to allow any country to use Laotian territory for military purposes or for interference in the internal affairs of other countries, and not to recognize the protection of any alliance or military coalition, including SEATO."

"The other Conference participants [including the United States] in response declare that 'they recognize and will respect and observe in every way the sovereignty, independence, neutrality, unity and territorial integrity' of Laos. They also bind themselves to specific undertakings" which are "self-explanatory" as they reflect their concomitant obligations. Furthermore, a Protocol provides details of the cease-fire agreed upon, withdrawal of foreign military personnel, and establishes an international Commission for supervision and control.

C.F. Salans, the attorney, Officer of the Legal Advisor, Department of State, herein quoted, concludes his description of the 1962 Laos settlement:

> The fact that the solutions to [extremely difficult] problems were reached [at the 1962 Conference on Laos], the nature of these solutions and the manner in which they were arrived at are matters which deserve study with a view to determining their applicability and relevance to other areas of international concern.
>
> At the same time it may be well to make a more cautious evaluation of the significance of the Laos Conference...The genuine desire [of the Soviet Union and the United States] to settle the Laos question at the conference table was manifest at Geneva...It thus seems fair to say at a minimum that, when a common purpose emerges, as it did regarding Laos, reconciliation of very divergent and conflicting views on how to achieve that end can be accomplished through negotiation and the conference technique.[149]

XI

Presidents Eisenhower and Kennedy Did Not "Commit" the United States to War Action in Vietnam.

The State Department Memorandum does injustice to presidents Eisenhower and Kennedy in quoting out of meaningful context certain of their statements and correspondence in support of a claim (Sec. II, C) that United States military war actions in South or North Vietnam are in fulfillment of their "assurances to the government of South Vietnam."

The Memorandum neglects to point out that President Eisenhower's letter of October 23, 1954 to Diem merely announced a willingness to open diplomatic negotiations for "a greater [United States] contribution to the welfare and stability" of Diem's regime, "*provided* that your Government is prepared to give assurances as to standards of performance it would be able to maintain in the event such aid were supplied" and only on condition that American "aid will be met by performance on the part of the Government of Vietnam in undertaking needed reforms."[150] Needless to say, there is not the slightest indication of any intention to violate the military provisions of the Geneva Accords, which had been adopted only three months earlier, and most assuredly there was not the slightest trace of a "commitment" to take war actions in Vietnam. President Eisenhower has stated categorically that his Administration made no commitment to South Vietnam "in terms of military support on any programs whatsoever."

President Kennedy insisted that the war in Vietnam was "their war" and promised only equipment and military advisers. His view of the United States commitment was summed up in a statement he made in September 1963:

> In the final analysis, it's their war. They're the ones who have to win or lose it. We can help them, give them equipment, we can send our men there as advisers but they have to win it.[151]

These "assurances" certainly do not add up to a commitment by the United States to take military action in Vietnam. The terms or concepts of "assurances" or "commitments" are not normal in the discourse of international or constitutional law. It is disturbing that the State Department should invoke the concept of such "commitment," and imply for it a legal content, especially as the conduct entailed is incompatible with the United Nations Charter and with the Geneva Accords.[152]

XII

To the Extent that the War Actions by the United States in Vietnam Violate International Treaties, They Also Violate the United States Constitution.

The United States Constitution considers ratified treaties to be the supreme law of the land and therefore considers any violation of such a treaty a violation also of the Constitution:

> This Constitution, and the laws of the United States which shall be made in pursuance thereof; and all treaties made, or which shall be made, under the authority of the United States, shall be the supreme law of the land. (Article VI (2))[153]

We have argued that the war actions of the United States in North and South Vietnam violate treaties to which the United States has become a party by due constitutional process. Above all, these war actions violate the Charter of the United Nations, of which the United States was a principal architect.

Because these actions violate the supreme law of the land, the question as to which branch of the Government may authorize them, or whether one branch of the Government may delegate to another branch legal powers to authorize them, becomes irrelevant. No branch of Government is permitted directly or indirectly (by delegation) to violate the Constitution.

Individual nations are bound by their international obligations toward other nations, *regardless* of their constitutional law. By disregarding international obligations a country acts in violation of international law, even if such a violation had been authorized by domestic law or by a domestic organ. Were this not the case, any country could liberate itself from its obligations toward the international community simply by domestic legislation or domestic decision.

In turn, changes in international practice may relieve nations from an international obligation; but such changes do not, by themselves, amend or alter domestic constitutions. The United States Constitution takes for granted the requirement of international law and comity that the grave act of entry into a war must be preceded by a formal declaration. As a matter of domestic law, the Constitution entrusts the power to make such a declaration exclusively to Congress. It has been contended that recent international practice indicates that a state of war may evolve without a prior declaration of war. This development on the international level would, of course, not change domestic law in respect to a requirement of a formal declaration.

Furthermore, the following observations concerned with the interrelation between international law and United States constitutional law are pertinent:

A. The interpretation at the Constitutional Convention 1787 of the Executive's Power to "repel sudden attack" (upon the United States) expresses the same principle as does the United Nations Charter regarding "self-defense" (on behalf of any Member of the United Nations).

The State Department Memorandum (Sec. IV, A) credits Madison and Gerry, at the Constitutional Convention 1787, with the explanation that the exclusive right of Congress "to declare war" leaves "to the Executive the power to repel sudden attacks"—as the Memorandum acknowledges, such a provision contemplated sudden attacks "probably...upon the United States."

The Memorandum further recites that, "It was objected [at the Constitutional Convention] that this might make it too easy for the Executive to involve the nation in war, but the motion carried." Here again, the State Department's arguments militate against its own conclusions. The Memorandum claims that this vote, in the light of Madison's and Gerry's clarification, implied the power of the Executive "to deploy American forces abroad and commit them to military operations..." Even Madison's and Gerry's explanation that the Executive may only repel sudden attacks upon the United States caused misgivings among the Founding Fathers. This, then, compels a restrictive interpretation of the power to "repel sudden attacks."

Above all, the Founding Fathers restricted the power of the Executive to "repel sudden attacks." This expresses and foreshadows the philosophy of the United Nations Charter provisions and affirms what is being urged here: namely, that just as the framers of the Constitution accepted the need for special, carefully restricted powers to "repel sudden attacks," so did the framers of the United Nations Charter (including the United States) acknowledge the need of Member states for special, carefully restricted powers "if an armed attack occurs." Hence, for such emergencies, the United States Constitution permits an exception to the general rule that only Congress can declare war; and the Charter permits an exception from its general rule that only the Security Council can authorize military actions if international peace is threatened. From the standpoint of both instruments, the Constitution and the Charter, exceptional emergency measures are permitted to prevent disaster.

B. Previous Deployment of United States Forces without Congressional Approval does not Provide a Valid Precedent in the Vietnam Case.

1. Objection must be registered to the State Department Memorandum's endeavor to represent 125 alleged precedents as germane to the Vietnam situation. The Memorandum asserts that since 1789, the President at least 125 times ordered "armed forces to take action *or* maintain position without prior Congressional authorization." Firstly, the figure—averaging almost

one such action every year—is reached by adding together (a) the mere dispatch of forces, (b) their dispatch for measures not involving combat and (c) their dispatch for combat. This last type of intervention totals but a fraction of 125. Secondly, except in Korea, none of these was in any way comparable in scale or duration with United States war actions in Vietnam. Thirdly, the Memorandum is unable to cite a single case in which the United States dispatched military forces for combat to a territory which, like South Vietnam, was "neutralized" by solemn international compact in the sense that it was in principle not to receive foreign military personnel or equipment and was not to ally itself with a foreign power and was not to permit foreign bases.

2. The main fallacy of the 125-case argument is that most of those measures were taken before international law increasingly prohibited such interventions (with or without declaration of war). The United Nations Charter as of 1945 definitively formulated new legal limits on the discretion of states to deploy force abroad. In no field has international law and the views concerning standards of permissible behavior changed more profoundly since 1787 than with regard to war. It is inappropriate to cite the protection of some United States Embassy buildings or fights against pirates in days gone by as precedents authorizing recourse to the unparalleled war actions in Vietnam during the 1960s.

3. Particularly inapposite, also, is the reference to President Truman's dispatch of troops to Korea. This action was in execution of a resolution of the Security Council. It was a "sanction" authorized by the competent organ of the United Nations, which sanctioning power, it can be maintained,[154] Congress by implication consented to by ratifying the United Nations Charter.

4. Actually, the "125-precedents" argument, when examined, puts into relief the unique and unprecedented character of the United States war actions in Vietnam. These war actions are unprecedented not only in their dimensions, their destructiveness and the ominous dangers they create for the United States, they are also unprecedented as regards the adverse legal circumstances (especially in the light of the United Nations Charter and the Geneva Accords) under which they occur.

5. In this connection, it is astonishing that the Memorandum (Sec. IV, B), in citing Article VI(2) of the Constitution, refers to SEATO but not to the Charter of the United Nations. Article VI(2) stipulates that:

> all treaties made...under the authority of the United States, shall be the supreme law of the land.

In these epoch-making words, the Constitution does indeed uphold the principle that no nation is above the law of nations. The Memorandum recognizes the binding quality of treaties only (and, as has been shown above, erroneously) with reference to SEATO. It fails to mention the United Nations Charter, which legally embodies the conscience of mankind, and is the most important treaty to which the United States is a party. Moreover, the SEATO Treaty itself prominently prescribes that it must be applied in conformity to the United Nations Charter.

6. It is not the case that the Charter puts undue restrictions upon American freedom of action. Regard for its letter and spirit is in the best interest of the United States. The Vietnam case illuminates the wisdom of the Charter and demonstrates vividly that circumvention of its essential provisions can lead to insoluble legal contradiction—and to moral, political and military difficulties of tragic proportions.

XIII

Conclusions

The foregoing analysis leads to the conclusion that the United States course of action in Vietnam violates fundamental rules of international law in several serious respects.

The policy of the United States in Vietnam has been to use military force in violation of the Geneva Accords of 1954, the United Nations Charter of 1945, the Kellogg-Briand Pact of 1928 and several rules of general international law. In the pursuit of this policy, the United States has ever more openly claimed for itself and the Saigon regime the right to consider the Geneva Accords of 1954, which regulate the internal and international position of the whole of Vietnam, as non-binding, while at the same time insisting that the other side is bound.

In particular, the following salient points emerge:

1. The United States claim to be acting in "collective self-defense" on behalf of South Vietnam is contrary to the well-established meaning of the rule laid down in Article 51 of the United Nations Charter to define the situations in which the right of collective self-defense may be lawfully exercised.

2. The United States military intervention in Vietnam therefore also violates the fundamental prohibition of the use of force

proclaimed in Article 2(4) of the Charter as a Principle of the United Nations.

3. The United States has refused for more than a decade to abide by the basic Charter obligation contained in Article 33(1) to seek the settlement of international disputes by peaceful means.

4. The United States has refused to make proper use of the elaborate machinery created by the Geneva Accords of 1954 for the purpose of preventing any improper developments in Vietnam. The United States, furthermore, abetted and supported the systematic disregard of these obligations by the Saigon regime.

5. The State Department contends that an armed attack by North Vietnam upon South Vietnam occurred before February 7, 1965, the date on which the United States started overt war actions. This contention itself implies that the use of force by the United States in Vietnam during the four-year period between 1961 and early 1965 was illegal. The State Department agrees with the position of this analysis that armed attack must have taken place to justify the use of force by the United States under the principle of "collective self-defense."

6. In February 1965, when the United States started war actions against North Vietnam, the United States formally declared that these war actions constituted *reprisals*. Under the rules of international law governing the right of reprisal, these war actions must be regarded as illegal reprisals.

7. The United States abetted the breach of the central provision of the Geneva Accords of 1954 by South Vietnam, namely, the obligation to hold nation-wide elections under international supervision looking toward the reunification of the southern and northern zones of Vietnam under a single government.

8. The United States also contravened other basic provisions of the Geneva Accords of 1954 by fostering a foreign military build-up in Vietnam and by virtually bringing South Vietnam into a military alliance.

9. The presence of large United States military forces in South Vietnam and the introduction of military equipment into South Vietnam has violated those provisions of the Geneva Accords

which prohibit any foreign military build-up in South Vietnam. This conclusion has been confirmed by findings of the ICC.

10. The war actions of the United States in South Vietnam are not authorized by the SEATO Treaty but, in fact, appear to be in violation of it.

11. Even if the United States were legally entitled to take war actions in Vietnam, its methods of warfare would still be illegal insofar as they have violated the rules and customs of warfare.

It should be emphasized that the present analysis does not suggest that Saigon's opponents in South or North Vietnam have abided by the Geneva Accords. The main argument here is that the United States and South Vietnam have not been entitled to respond to these contraventions as they did. The actions of the United States and the Saigon regime have vitiated their own legal position by contravening the most basic provisions of the international settlement of the eight-year French-Vietnamese war (the Geneva Accords of 1954): (a) the obligation not to militarize the south; and (b) the obligation to unify the two temporary zones of Vietnam by July 1956. If the elections for reunification had been duly held, the tragic developments that resulted from the continued separation of the two temporary zones might have been avoided altogether.

The tenor and logic of the State Department Memorandum of March 4, 1966 provokes a concern that exceeds the conflict in Vietnam. Its manner of interpreting facts and its interpretations of international law pose serious dangers for the future. We consider that it is a professional duty to oppose the acceptance of the reasoning and principal conclusions contained in the State Department Memorandum.

The logic of the Memorandum challenges the basis of world legal order by weakening the foundations of the United Nations with respect to the regulation of force used by nations.

The United States has acted in disregard of the principles and purposes set forth in the United Nations Charter. The United States has abandoned the standards and procedures of international law to such an extent as to imply that "international law is irrelevant in the Vietnam case."

But the tragedy in Vietnam reveals that the rules of law, when so flagrantly disregarded, have a way of reasserting the calm wisdom underlying their creation. If international law had been followed, both Vietnam and the American people would have been spared what Secretary General U Thant has described as "one of the most barbarous wars in history." The mounting dangers connected with the military involvement of the United States in Vietnam suggest that a reversal of policy is not only demanded by law, but follows from the elemental counsels of prudence. It is misrepresenting the situation to suppose that the only choice available to the United States is either the continuation of the war or "abject defeat." For a nation to revise or even to repudiate a wrong course of action involves a less damaging loss of prestige than does its continuation.[155] The existing system of world order has developed a storehouse of procedural and institutional devices that can be invoked to end the fighting and, thereafter, to reach toward a constructive solution based on the restoration of the Geneva Accords.

The first and most urgent task is for all sides to de-escalate their participation in the war and to avoid further devastation. The first step must be initiated by the United States, since the United States is the state most actively engaged in these war actions. Above all, the United States has monopolized control of the airspace over both North and South Vietnam. The termination of aerial bombardment, at least north of the seventeenth parallel, appears to be a firm prerequisite to the opening of peace negotiations.

The history of hostilities in international life also seems to show that it is the actual antagonists who must participate in cease-fire negotiations. The reluctance of the United States to declare unambiguously its readiness to negotiate with the NLF is unfortunate in this respect. However dependent the NLF may be on the Hanoi regime, it is extremely unlikely that an agreement settling the conflict will be effective unless the NLF is bound by it. The NLF cannot be bound by an agreement to which it is not a party—even assuming that North Vietnam would agree to accept obligations on behalf of the NLF. In the case of the Geneva Accords of 1954 the French were able to bind also the successor regime in Saigon, as they expressly did, because the French possessed the constitutional authority to do so. But neither the United States nor the Democratic Republic of Vietnam can bind the NLF to uphold arrangements to which it has not given formal assent.

Historical experience also indicates that a belligerent who has not been defeated will refuse to enter negotiations unless he understands the war aims of the opponent and believes that the opponent's war aims form a tolerable basis for negotiations. The assertions of President Johnson, Secretary of State Rusk and Ambassador Goldberg are hopeful to the extent that they affirm a desire by the United States to return to the Geneva Accords of 1954. But these declarations are incompatible with other authoritative statements made on behalf of the United States, seemingly made in the same breath, and are dramatically incompatible with actual United States policies. The continuous and systematic intensification of warfare, the systematic construction of vast and costly military bases in South Vietnam, the preparations for the dispatch to Vietnam of additional hundreds of thousands of United States forces, the frequent assertions that the United States is prepared to continue the war for many years to come, the failure to repudiate clearly Marshal Ky's demand for an invasion of North Vietnam are among the contradictions between the words and deeds of the United States Government. These contradictions must be reduced considerably before negotiations can be expected to take place.

In conclusion, we urge that the Government of the United States re-examine its military involvement in the light of the international legal order. It is our belief that a conscientious and impartial re-examination will establish the illegality of the current United States position in Vietnam and that it will further reveal that it is in the short-term and long-term interest of the United States to bring these policies into conformity with international law. We urge that this effort proceed as a matter of urgent national necessity.

Consultative Council of the
Lawyers Committee on
American Policy Towards Vietnam

Richard A. Falk	Saul H. Mendlovitz
John H. E. Fried	Richard S. Miller
Richard J. Barnet	Hans J. Morgenthau
John H. Herz	William G. Rice
Stanley Hoffmann	Burns H. Weston
Wallace McClure	Quincy Wright

The signers of this legal analysis agree with its general tenor and conclusions, although not necessarily with every formulation that it contains.

Notes

1. The Department of State alludes to these reactions in the opening paragraphs of its White Book of February 1965: "The war in Vietnam is a new kind of war, a fact as yet poorly understood in most parts of the world. Much of the confusion that prevails in the thinking of many people, and even many governments, stems from this basic misunderstanding..." *Aggression from the North*, DEP'T OF STATE RELEASE 7839, Far Eastern Series 130, p. 1 (1965).

2. See Lawyers Committee on American Towards Vietnam, *American Policy Vis-a-Vis Vietnam*, Memorandum of Law; reproduced in CONG. REC. of September 23, 1965.

3. Senator William Proxmire, inserting the State Department Memorandum into the *Congressional Record*, declared:

> ...because we are a country which believes in ...a world of law, as well as a nation of law, it is important that we be precisely certain as to what justification in law there is. CONG. REC. 5274-79 (March 10, 1966).

4. See *Indochina: A Brief Background Statement*, LIBRARY OF CONGRESS, LEG. REF. SERIES (DS 550) 7 (1950).

5. JEAN LACOUTURE, VIETNAM: BETWEEN TWO TRUCES 61 (1966).

6. The agreement stated that the "free state" of Vietnam formed "part of the Indochinese Federation and the French Union." For Text of Agreement of March 6, 1946 see VIETNAM: HISTORY, DOCUMENTS AND OPINIONS ON A MAJOR WORLD CRISIS 61 (Gettleman, ed. 1965). [Hereafter cited as GETTLEMAN.]

7. See DAVID HALBERSTAM, THE MAKING OF A QUAGMIRE 60 (1964).

8. Statement by Secretary of State Dean Acheson, May 8, 1950. DEP'T OF STATE BULL. 821 (May 22, 1950); reproduced in GETTLEMAN, 89.

9. 30 DEP'T OF STATE BULL. 539-40 (April 12, 1954); quoted in GETTLEMAN 89-91.

10. An emergency session of the Churchill Cabinet rejected on April 25, 1954 a United States proposal that, on the basis of a common declaration by the United States, the United Kingdom, France, the Philippines and the

Associated States, "U.S. naval aircraft would go into action at Dien Bien Phu on April 28." Mr. Eden commented on the United States proposal in his "Memoirs"; "If the United Kingdom acceded to this latest American proposal, we should be supporting direct U.S. intervention in the Indochina war and, probably, later American action against the Chinese mainland. His Majesty's Government consequently decided to reject the American proposal ..." THE MEMOIRS OF ANTHONY EDEN: FULL CIRCLE 119 (1960). See also pp. 89-160 regarding United States attitudes before and during the Geneva Conference, including United States proposals advocating the use of force.

11. Chalmers M. Roberts, "The Day We Didn't Go to War," *The Reporter*, Sept. 14, 1954, pp. 31-5. Cambodia, the Democratic Republic of Vietnam, France, Laos, the People's Republic of China, the State of Vietnam, the Soviet Union, the United Kingdom and the United States participated in the Geneva Conference.

12. For example, IAN BROWNLIE, INTERNATIONAL LAW AND THE USE OF FORCE BY STATES 273 (1963): "any proviso, implied or express, as to self-defense was understood to be an exceptional right, a privilege"; many authorities are cited by Brownlie to support this conclusion.

13. The assertion of a pre-existing right to the unilateral use of force in self-defense except under specific safeguards is, for example, contradicted by the findings and proposals of the "Harvard Research in International Law"—the authoritative project on the subject of self-defense undertaken in the United States in the 1930s under the auspices of the Harvard Law School.

After a four-year study, this eminent group did not propose to grant any unilateral right of self-defense or co-defense under any circumstances; thus, they did not even make the exception embodied in Article 51 for the emergency of "armed attack." Instead, they proposed that no "aggression" be deemed to exist, and hence no right of self-defense or co-defense could exist until illegal resort to "armed force" had been duly determined by a proper procedure (*e.g.* the League of Nations, the World Court, etc.) to which the alleged "aggressor" State had previously agreed. These experts followed the clear trend of the then existing international law. They emphasized that treaties like the Kellogg-Briand Pact of 1928 and the Covenant of the League of 1920 were "characteristic" and "typical" of "the period since 1920" and that, furthermore, "like provisions [prohibition of force without prior exhaustion of pacific settlement procedures] may [also] be found in treaties of earlier periods." Hence, they pointed out that to make any response to alleged aggression conditional on impartial determination of illegality was "the result of a long historical evolution; it would be erroneous to connect it solely with such instruments as the Covenant of the League and the Pact of Paris" [the Kellogg-Briand Pact]. 33 AM. J. INT'L L. 871, 899, 823-4 Supp. (1939).

14. 7 JOHN BASSETT MOORE, DIGEST OF INTERNATIONAL LAW 919 (1906).

15. Philip C. Jessup, Judge of the International Court of Justice and eminent international lawyer, has urged an even stricter limitation of the right of self-defense than is implied in Webster's definition, but calls the latter "accurate ...in the sense that the exceptional right of self-defense can be exercised only if the end cannot be otherwise obtained." He insists that only an armed attack causing "the necessary degree of immediacy and urgency" justifies self-defense—that is, even "individual self-defense." JESSUP, A MODERN LAW OF NATIONS 163-64 (1948).

Similarly, the treatise by Oppenheim-Lauterpacht states that: "Only such acts of violence in the interest of self-preservation are excused as are necessary in self-defense ...otherwise ...a violation of another State on the part of the endangered State ...is not excused and justified"—quoting Webster's definition, (1 INTERNATIONAL LAW 298, 8th ed., 1955):

> " ...the right of self-defense—conceived as an inherent, a natural right—gives the States resorting to it ...[only] the right to decide in the first instance, when there is *periculum in mora*, whether they are in the presence of an armed attack calling for armed resistance. Unless it is to become an occasion for license and lawlessness, an inherent right must be controlled and accountable to a higher authority—provided that the authority is in a position to act effectively in accordance with its constitution. The clear terms of Article 51 adequately express that general principle of jurisprudence." (2 OPPENHEIM-LAUTERPACHT, INTERNATIONAL LAW 159, 7th ed., 1952.) In Vol. I, 1955, p. 299, this standard work repeats the warning that otherwise "the notion of self-preservation" can be "used as a cloak for concealing deliberate breaches." [Hereafter cited as OPPENHEIM-LAUTERPACHT.]

The third work quoted by the Memorandum, DEREK W. BOWETT, SELF DEFENSE IN INTERNATIONAL LAW 142-44 (1958), accepts Mr. Webster's definition in connection with the Nuremberg judgment.

16. In May 1964, the State Department did not yet assert an armed attack:

> " ...the disciplined leadership, direction and support from North Vietnam is a critical factor in the strength of the Viet Cong movement" but the Viet Cong receives "large indigenous support." Bureau of Public Affairs, DEP'T OF STATE, No. 6 *Foreign Affairs Outline* (May 1964).

A year later, Marcus Raskin, co-Director of the Institute for Policy Studies, characterized the conflict as a civil war, in which "ninety per cent or more of the rebels' weapons come from captured U.S. or South Vietnamese store depots or the black market" (Marcus Raskin, *A Citizens' White Paper on American Policy in Vietnam and Southeast Asia*, p. 10; inserted by Congressman William Fitts Ryan in the CONG. REC. at 9255 (May 5, 1965)).

On January 25, 1966, General Wallace M. Greene, Jr., Commandant of the United States Marine Corps, referred to the "Viet Cong's support from the north," but avoided calling it an armed attack. (Speech before the Union League Club of New York, in Cong. Rec. 1441-42 (Feb. 1, 1966).)

In the April 1966 issue of *Foreign Affairs*, "The Faceless Viet Cong," George A. Carver, Jr. concludes an analysis strongly supporting the United States policy: "The current struggle in South Vietnam is an historically rooted, political phenomenon of infinite complexity, particularly since it involves an externally [North Vietnam] directed Communist drive for power interlaced with a genuine indigenous [South Vietnamese] social revolution."

17. *"The Vietnam Conflict: The Substance and The Shadow"*; Report submitted to the Senate Foreign Relations Committee, January 6, 1966. [Hereafter cited as the MANSFIELD REPORT.]

18. For example, League of Nations Special Committee's *Commentary on the Definition ...of Aggression* (September, 1923), reprinted in 5 WHITEMAN, DIGEST OF INTERNATIONAL LAW at 730 (1965); Clyde Eagleton, "The Attempt to Define Aggression," INTERNATIONAL CONCILIATION (November, 1930); and see *Act Relating to the Definition of the Aggressor*, 5 WHITEMAN at 734.

19. During the San Francisco Conference, the United States Joint Chiefs of Staff informed the U.S. Delegation that they wished to make regional enforcement action (at least outside the Western Hemisphere) dependent on previous authorization by the Security Council to enable the United States to exercise a veto. "In view of the attitude of the Joint Chiefs toward American security interests in the Western Pacific and their concern over potential Anglo-Soviet conflict in Europe ...they may have wanted...to retain a possible American veto on actions in parts of the world outside the Western Hemisphere." RUTH B. RUSSELL, A HISTORY OF THE UNITED NATIONS CHARTER 698 NOTE 12 (1958).

20. HANS KELSEN, LAW OF THE UNITED NATIONS 798 (1950).

21. *Id.* at 799-800.

22. JESSUP, *op. cit. supra* note 15, at 205.

23. BOWETT, *op. cit. supra* note 15, at 180-81.

24. MANSFIELD REPORT at 2.

Also instructive is the report by Senator Allen J. Ellender on his investigations in Saigon on behalf of the Senate Committee on Appropriations at the end of 1961:

"Nov. 29, 1961 ...Some of our representatives here state that there have been quite a few people to infiltrate since 1959. Some say that South Vietnam is in a much better condition economically, and that some of the infiltration results from this condition.

I hesitate to discuss all the information obtained from our representatives here, although much of it is not classified. My fear is that the cry of 'Communism' is being used to pull our leg. Since the time when Diem was first elected there are two areas in South Vietnam where some opposition to him has developed and remains adamant in opposing him. One area is in the southern part of the country and the other northwesterly of Saigon. The people of these areas permit, in fact, invite, I was told, some infiltration from the north in order to strengthen their opposition to Diem. In Saigon, also, there are many dissidents who do not like President Diem's tactics ...It is my belief that much of the trouble stems from within ...[reference to charges of corruption] ...

There is still much poverty, and the few dissidents and complainants can whip up much sympathy ...

Gen. Howard K. Eggleston heads our MAAG [Military Assistance Advisory Group] here. He gave me quite a briefing on the situation here. Much of the trouble comes from within, as I said before. We are trying to deal with the guerrilla problem,that is, more and more emphasis is being applied to that phase of military training ...It seems as though the more we spend, the more trouble develops ...If a careful, unbiased and unprejudiced appraisal of the present situation were made, I believe that much of the trouble now occurring stems from within. Some feel we should send American troops here. I would not do so under any circumstances ..." (87th Cong., 2nd Sess., Senate Doc. 73, *Report of U.S. Foreign Policy and Appropriations*. By Hon. Allen J. Ellender, U.S. Senator from Louisiana. (1962, 137-142.)

25. MANSFIELD REPORT at 1. Senator Mansfield's Address at Yeshiva University is reproduced in the CONG. REC., Senate, June 16, 1966, 12856-58.

The statement in his address that when the sharp increase in the American military effort began in early 1965, only about 400 North Vietnamese soldiers were estimated to be among the enemy forces in the south, was confirmed by the U.S. Department of Defense (Ted Knap, *Daily News*, Washington, D.C., June 23, 1966).

26. KELSEN, *op. cit. supra* note 20, at 797.

27. JULIUS STONE, LEGAL CONTROLS OF INTERNATIONAL CONFLICT 245 (1954); see also pp. 264-265.

28. Mr. Lleras-Camargo (Colombia): "The Latin American countries understood, as Senator Vandenberg had said, that the origin of the term 'collective security' is identified with the necessity of preserving regional systems like the Latin-American one ...If a group of countries with regional ties declare their solidarity for their mutual defense, as in the case of the American states, they will undertake such defense jointly if and when one of them is attacked." "[T]he delegates of Mexico, Costa Rica, Paraguay, Venezuela, Chile, Ecuador, Bolivia, Panama, Uruguay, Peru, Guatemala,

El Salvador, Brazil, Honduras, and Cuba associated themselves with this statement." Quoted in 5 WHITEMAN, *op. cit. supra* note 18, at 1073; RUSSELL, *op. cit. supra* note 19, at 704.

It is universally recognized that the provision pertaining to collective self-defense was inserted into the Charter to permit collective actions only under "appropriate" regional arrangements, such as the "Pan American Union [which] for 50 years had represented the finest flower of international cooperation for security by peaceful means"—as declared by Senator Vandenberg, whereupon "the Latin cheers took the roof off." *Id.* at 711-12.

It is true that Article 51 was eventually inserted in the Charter at the end of Chapter VII ("Actions with respect to Threats to the Peace ..."), immediately prior to Chapter VIII ("Regional Arrangements"), and that therefore collective self-defense is permitted if other Charter requirements are fulfilled, in contexts other than regional arrangements. But this fact in no way undermines the narrow interpretation of the "inherent" right of collective self-defense insisted upon by those who framed the Charter.

29. M.S. AMOS, REMEDIES FOR WAR 60 (1880); quoted in 6 MOORE, DIGEST OF INTERNATIONAL LAW 3-4 (1906).

30. Article 2 of Kellogg-Briand Pact, 1928 in *U.S. Statutes at Large,*XXXXVI, p. 2343.

31. *Asylum Case* (Colombia vs. Peru), Judgment of Nov. 20, 1950, INTERNATIONAL COURT OF JUSTICE REPORTS 206, 285 (1950).

32. Article III of the Treaty prohibits not only armed intervention ("collective self-defense") but even diplomatic intervention. Article III then lists the policies "authorized by international law" which third states may pursue "in their character as neutrals":

> [They] undertake to make every effort for the maintenance of peace. To that end they will adopt in their character as neutrals a common and solidary attitude; they will exercise the political, juridical or economic means authorized by international law; they will bring the influence of public opinion to bear.

The Treaty was signed by Argentina, Brazil, Chile, Mexico, Paraguay, the United States and Uruguay. It was ratified by the United States on June 15, 1934. See also CONG. REC., 73rd Cong., 2d Sess., Vol. LXXVIII, at 11910.

33. BOWETT, *op. cit. supra* note 15, at 216-18.

34. For example, if in 1965, during the Kashmir conflict, Pakistan, claiming armed attack by India, had requested collective assistance from China, and China had thereupon bombed India, the United States would have considered this a *causus belli* against China, with possibly serious consequences also for Pakistan.

35. It is important to note that the United Nations General Assembly and the United States considered the rival Hungarian Government,

which demanded withdrawal of Soviet troops, as legitimate although this was a revolutionary, insurrectionist regime.

36. A report on Southeast Asia issued February 25, 1963 by a bipartisan Senate group headed by Senator Mike Mansfield stated: "It is most disturbing that after seven years of the republic, South Vietnam appears ...more removed from, rather than closer to, the achievement of popularly responsible and responsive government." *Vietnam and Southeast Asia*, reprinted as appendix in MANSFIELD REPORT, *op. cit. supra* note 24, at 18-32.

37. *New York Times Magazine*, Sept. 18, 1966, pp. 119-20.

38. Elections Speech of September 28, 1964; quoted in *New York. Herald Tribune*, March 20, 1966, p. 14.

39. In March 1963, when approximately 12,000 United States military personnel were in South Vietnam, and United States combat actions were still two years away, a group of 62 prominent Americans publicly called attention to United States aggressivity in Vietnam:

> The more aggressively [the United States] pursues the war, the more money, planes, tanks, guns and military personnel it pours into South Vietnam, the more Diem looks like an American puppet. Every time American planes, manned by American 'advisors' and Diem soldiers paid U.S. handouts, bomb a peasant village, burn a peasant's rice hoard, kill a peasant's water buffalo or drive a peasant from his ancestral land, the Viet Cong gets more sympathy and more recruits from the local population. More and more, as death and destruction increase, the issue becomes, in the eyes of the Vietnamese people, that of American interference and control versus Vietnamese independence and self-determination ..." "Open Letter to President Kennedy" signed by 62 Americans, published in *Washington Post*, March 1, 1963.

Regarding the present situation, Thich Nhat Hanh, the Director of the School for Social Studies in Saigon, has written:

> If the United states wants to escalate the war, nothing that the Vietnamese can do will matter. A change of government will make no difference. The war will go on. (*New York Review of Books*, June 9, 1966, p. 4.)

40. *New York Times*, April 10, 1966, pp. E-1, E-9.

41. Quoted in 5 WHITEMAN, *op. cit. supra* note 18, at 1071.

42. Department of External Affairs, REPORT ON THE UNITED NATIONS CONFERENCE ON INTERNATIONAL ORGANIZATION, 41, repeated at 41-2 (Ottawa, 1945).

43. STONE, *op. cit. supra* note 27, at 244; see also, *e.g.*, JESSUP, *op. cit. supra* note 15, at 168.

44. S.C.O.R. 790th Meeting, p. 5.—The reference to "collective security" was evidently to "collective self-defense" under Article 51. For, the fact that "collective security" (in the meaning of military sanctions autho-

rized by the Security Council under Chapter VII of the Charter) is available also to non-Members, was then fully established by the Korean precedent.

45. U.N. YEARBOOK 1000 (1950); Annex at 994.

46. *Id.* at 902, 890, 934. In fact, the 1947 conference at which "Vietnam" became a WMO charter member, and the 1950 FAO conference which made "Vietnam" an FAO member, took place in Washington, D.C.

47. U.N. YEARBOOK 884, 894, 945 (1951).

48. S/3881 and 3885, S.C.O.R. Supp. [July-Sept. 1957] pp. 34-5, 37. Ambassador Lodge also pleaded for Vietnam's unification at the Security Council session on September 7, 1957. "No one can deny the historic, cultural and racial ties which bind [the people of Vietnam] together as a nation. Few would deny them the right of nationhood ..." Mr. Lodge reproached the Soviet Union for preventing the unification elections so that Vietnam is "still divided." Thus he upheld the pledge, on behalf of the United States, regarding these elections (S.C.O.R., 790th meeting).

49. MARCUS RASKIN and BERNARD FALL, ed., THE VIETNAM READER 378 (1965). It was "Vietnam," under the name of "State of Vietnam" (represented by the Bao Dai regime) that signed for example, a Mutual Defense Assistance Agreement with the United States on December 23, 1950, and co-signed the Japanese Peace Treaty on September 8, 1951. In addition to the United States and the United Kingdom, "twenty-five Western nations guardedly recognized Vietnam in 1950 as an Associated State of the French Union." EDEN, *op. cit. supra* note 10, at 89.

50. According to George A. Carver Jr., permanent NLF missions exist in Havana, Peking, Moscow, Prague, East Berlin, Budapest, Cairo, Djakarta and Algiers. Op. *cit. supra* note 16, at 367.

51. Statement of November 8, 1956, quoted in *International Law and the Middle East Crisis*, a symposium of papers originally delivered at the Regional Meeting of the American Society of International Law, Tulane University, April 6, 1957.

52. *New York Times*, November 6, 1956.

53. These safeguards were strengthened by the *Uniting for Peace Resolution*, which permitted the General Assembly to step into the breach also on behalf of non-Members if the Security Council is stalemated.

54. At this time the question has become academic, as membership is almost universal. "The phrasing of Article 51 ...suggests that it was due to the assumption that membership in the U.N. would be practically universal." 2 OPPENHEIM-LAUTERPACHT, at 155, note 20.

55. Another example of such evolution is the established practice of the Security Council, contrary to the strict wording of Article 27(3), to consider a Resolution carried even if a permanent Member of the Council

does not cast an affirmative vote but abstains. See e.g., EUGENE P. CHASE, THE UNITED NATIONS IN ACTION 384 (1950).

56. The Memorandum refrains from raising the argument that the United States is perhaps not bound by, or not bound to respect, the Geneva Declaration. The argument would not be very persuasive. It would be difficult for a state to justify, as does the Memorandum, destructive bombings on the grounds of violations of a compact by the other side, while at the same time denying that the bombing state is itself bound. Furthermore, it is an undisputed principle of international as well as domestic law, that C cannot disturb an agreement between A, B, D and E on the pretext that he, C, is not party to their agreement.

Finally, the fact that the United States did not sign the Declaration of July 21, 1954 is irrelevant, since none of the Conference participants signed it; instead, they agreed to it by putting formal voice votes on record. (See GETTLEMAN 154-159.) "It matters not whether a treaty is made orally or in writing ..." (I OPPENHEIM-LAUTERPACHT, 898.)

The fact that the Geneva Accords are binding upon the United States was also asserted by the Chairman of the Committee on Peace and Law through the United Nations of the American Bar Association. EBERHARD P. DEUTSCH, "The Legality of the U.S. Position in Vietnam," *A.B.A.J.* 440 (1966).

57. The fact that the 17th parallel was a military and a provisional military demarcation line is stated in the title of Chapter I of the Armistice Agreement, repeated eight times in its first eight Articles and unequivocally reiterated in the multi-nation Declaration.

58. See 1st and 2nd Reports, Cmd. 9461, para 118.

59.

> Apart from the demonstrations [in Saigon] against the Geneva Agreement on 20th July 1955, which degenerated into violence against the two hotels, Majestic and Galliani, where Commission personnel were staying ...the political attitude of the State of Vietnam to the Geneva Accords and its effect on ...the implementation of the Vietnam Agreement require very early consideration. 4th Report of the ICC [for period April 11 to August 10, 1955], Cmd. 9654, para. 44.

> On October 18, 1955, Bao Dai ...revoked the full powers which he had given to [Diem]. In a proclamation to the people of Vietnam, he said: "I would no longer lend my name and my law to someone who will lure you into ruin, famine and war." (Quoted by W. WARBEY, VIETNAM: THE TRUTH 63 (London, 1965).

However, five days later (Oct. 23, 1955), a "referendum" in South Vietnam substituted Diem as Head of State in place of Bao Dai.

60. "How the French Got out of Vietnam," *New York Times Magazine*, May 2, 1965; reproduced in Raskin & Fall, *op. cit. supra* note 49, at 81-95. The police methods of the regime are illustrated by the South

Vietnam Decree Law 093-SLCT of February 1, 1964, as amended in May 1965, which, for example, decrees heaviest punishment for "All plots and actions under the false name of peace and neutrality according to a Communist policy and similar plots and actions." Full text in PEACE IN VIETNAM, *Report Prepared for the American Friends Service Committee* 104-5 (1966).

61. For example, the 7th Interim Report for the period starting August 1, 1956, refers to "three complaints" from the Diem regime and "32 petitions ...from individuals involving 35 incidents alleging murder, arrest and confiscation of property" in the north; and to "194 complaints" from the northern regime and "320 petitions from individuals, involving 1047 incidents alleging murder, detention, arrest, confiscation of property, etc ...involving large numbers of persons" in the south.

The latter complaints and petitions referred especially to actions taken under Diem's notorious Order of January 6, 1956, mentioned above: "reprisals against individuals and organizations under the 'Campaign of Denunciation of Communists' ..." There were even "a few complaints alleging that persons asking for a Consultative Conference with a view to holding general elections [for unification] were being arrested or detained by" the Diem regime (para. 19; see p*assim*, and 6th Interim Report, covering period December 11, 1955—July 31, 1956, paras. 21, 25-26).

The Commission's inquiries about "the results of the trials and other actions taken by the [Diem] Government under Article 22 [of the Cease-Fire Agreement, requiring that persons who violate the Agreement's provisions on democratic freedoms be "suitably punished"] were left unanswered" by the Diem regime (para. 23).

In its 7th Report, the ICC also protests against South Vietnam's decision altogether "not to send any more replies to the Commission's communications" regarding violations of democratic freedoms (Article 14(c), Armistice Agreement) and "not to permit the deployment of any [ICC] Mobile Teams for investigation of complaints under that Article in South Vietnam" (para. 60).

62. Namely, an international commission composed of Canada, India and Poland. At the closing session of the Conference, the United States expressed preference for supervision of the elections by the United Nations. In any case, the election commission agreed upon in the Accords was to consist of three Members of the United Nations, and was not supposed to be identical with the ICC. Its machinery, personnel, rules, mode of operations, etc. were still to be decided upon, and South Vietnam also could and should have requested any safeguards it desired in these respects.

63.

> Historical evidence of who began violating the agreement first is hard to come by. But it is certain that the most significant violation was the refusal of ...Diem

> ...to proceed with the elections ... [H]e refused to enter into the discussions called for in the agreement to fix the details ...This gross violation was viewed not with "grave concern" by us but with great approval.
>
> ...Undoubtedly, the Viet Minh under Ho Chi Minh would have won such a free election. President Eisenhower declares in his *Mandate for Change* that all the experts he talked to in that period believed Ho would get at least 80 per cent of the vote. Ho was the nationalist patriot of Vietnam who had our favor and our help in World War II when he organized local resistance to the Japanese occupation ...
>
> ...the purpose of the 1954 Accord was to end the fighting ...whereas we and our agent, Diem, frustrated that purpose by refusing to allow the election to proceed. (Senator Wayne Morse, Remarks at St. Mary's University, San Antonio, Texas, May 1965; quoted in GETTLEMAN 281-2.)

64. On May 8, 1956, the co-Chairmen in a joint message to Saigon and Hanoi

> strongly urged both the Governments in Vietnam ...to ensure the implementation of the political provisions ...of the Final Declaration ...[and] requested the two Governments to transmit their views about the time required for the opening of consultations on the organization of elections and the time required for holding of elections to unify Vietnam.

Simultaneously the co-Chairmen directed the ICC

> to persevere in its efforts to maintain and strengthen peace in Vietnam on the basis of the fulfillment of the Geneva Agreements on Vietnam with a view to the reunification of the country through the holding of elections under the supervision of an International Commission.

Thereupon, the ICC stated that it

> will, as directed by the co-Chairmen ...persevere in its efforts to maintain and strengthen peace in Vietnam on the basis of the fulfillment of the Geneva Agreements on Vietnam with a view to the reunification of the country through the holding of elections in Vietnam under the supervision of an International Commission. (Para. 86, 90, Sixth Interim Report of ICC, reprinted in "Supplemental Foreign Assistance. Fiscal Year 1966-Vietnam." *Hearings before the Committee on Foreign Relations*. U.S. Senate, 89th Congr., 2d Sess. on S. 2793, pt. 1, at 730 (1966). [Hereafter cited as 1966 HEARINGS]).

Diem defied these appeals as he had systematically defied the ICC, the co-Chairmen, and (insofar as they imposed obligations on his regime) the Geneva Accords in general. The contention in the State Department Memorandum that if Hanoi felt aggrieved by the failure to hold the elections then it should perhaps have appealed to the co-Chairmen (note 10), is rather unconvincing, as is its advice that Hanoi's "remedies lay in discussion with Saigon." Despite continuous complaints from North Vietnam and urgings by the ICC, Saigon sabotaged the bilateral "joint Commission," which was specifically set up by the Accords for direct consultations between the two sides and was, as the ICC insisted, "an important part of the machinery for the implementation of the Geneva Agreements." In fact, because of Diem's attitude, the Joint Commission became defunct after the dissolution of the French High Command in May 1956. See ICC Seventh Report, para. 65.

North Vietnam did, in fact, endeavor through the ICC and otherwise, to have the elections held even after 1956. For example, in 1958 Ho Chi Minh visited Prime Minister Nehru of India in order to solicit his support for such action.

In any case, even assuming that North Vietnam did not utilize all remedies open to it to protest violations by the south, this failure would not legalize violations by the south.

65. Virtually identical statements were made in the ICC's Seventh Report, dated July 12, 1957, para. 66; 8th Report, dated June 5, 1958, para. 43; 9th Report, dated March 10, 1959, para. 45; 10th Report, dated April 6, 1960, para. 68. All these Reports are reproduced in 1966 HEARINGS at 731-6.

66. CARVER, JR., *op. cit. supra* note 16, at 357.

67. DEP'T OF STATE BULL., Vol. L, No. 1297, at 690 (May 4, 1964). The statement omits the essential point that the partition was limited to two years, and that a "Republic of South Vietnam" has never existed.

68. Quoted from CONG. REC. of Aug. 6, 1964, in 1966 HEARINGS at 55-6.

69. U.S. White Paper, DEP'T OF STATE PUBL. 7308, pt. I, at 3-4 (Dec. 1961).

70. George Kahin & John Lewis, "The United States in Vietnam," *Bulletin of the Atomic Scientists*, June 1965, pp. 80-1.

71. The same point is made in PEACE IN VIETNAM, *op. cit. supra* note 60, at 43.

72. Since the permission is only for "man-to-man rotation" by either "party ...of its armed forces," and since only France and the Democratic Republic of Vietnam were the parties to the Cease-Fire Agreement, it is highly debatable whether the replacement of French personnel by United States personnel was within the letter or spirit of the Agreement.

73. Between Aug. 1, 1955 and April 30, 1956, the ICC "was seized with 96 cases which may have violated Article 16 [Ban on introduction of foreign military personnel] and 114 cases which may have violated Article 17 [Ban on introduction of war materials] in South Vietnam"—altogether 210 cases—but was not seized with any such case regarding North Vietnam, "as there was no team report, notification or complaint, warranting such consideration." 7th Report, para, 50.

74. Certain other clandestine activities, such as the role of the CIA within the framework of the University of Michigan program in South Vietnam, became known in 1966.

75. Special Report, dated June 2, 1962, paras. 12-13, reproduced in 1966 HEARINGS, at 739-40.

76. The Polish delegation dissented from the findings of the Indian-Canadian majority that the north had violated the Geneva Accords (see para. 10 of the Special Report).

77. Homer Bigart, "U.S. Helps Vietnam in Test against Guerrillas," *New York Times*, March 29, 1962, pp. 1 ff.: "First comprehensive plan to pacify South Vietnam ...the operation is subsidized directly with U.S. money, military planning and technical aid ...In this region ["rubber plantation near Bencat"] 1,200 families are to be removed voluntarily or forcibly ...the abandoned villages will be burned to deprive theViet Cong of shelter and food."

78. "Weed Killers Aid War onViet Cong. They are Used to Destroy Reds' Shelters and Crops," *New York Times*, March 28, 1965, p. 2. This newspaper account also states:

> U.S. Air Force crews have flown C-123 cargo planes with internal chemical tanks that feed spray devices under the wings.
>
> ...Depending upon the mixture and concentration, however, these [defoliant] chemical compounds may be used to destroy many kinds of plant life ...Until now, on the premise that the United States has not been engaged directly in the war against theViet Cong, U.S. planes have been kept out of crop damage operations. The South Vietnamese Air Force, however, has swooped on areas believed to be under cultivation by theViet Cong and has sprayed them with heavy defoliant concentrates. Such operations have been the subject of controversy. Many officials ...cite occasional errors, in which crops grown by loyal South Vietnamese civilians have been ruined. Moreover, the operations are said to leave the United States open to charges of germ warfare, even if unjustified. The uproar over the use of riot-control gas is cited in support of this argument.

79. *New York Times*, February 5, 1965, pp. 1-4. The article also stated, "independent analysts here [in Saigon] believe these [North Vietnamese] peace terms [discussed by Mr. Kosygin in Hanoi] could be packaged at a conference in such a way as to allow the U.S. a face-saving exit from South Vietnam. They say time would thus be bought as it was at the Conference on Laos."

80. *New York Times*, February 7, 1965, pp. 1-4.

81. *New York Times*, February 8, 1965, p. 15.

82. The statement described the reasons and extent of the reprisals as follows:

> Commencing at 2 A.M. on Feb. 7 Saigon time, 2 South Vietnamese air fields, 2 U.S. barracks areas, several villages and one town in South Vietnam were subjected to deliberate surprise attacks. Substantial casualties resulted. Moreover, these attacks were only made possible by the continuing infiltration of personnel and equipment from North Vietnam. These infiltrations markedly increased during 1964 and continue to increase. To meet these attacks, the Government of South Vietnam and the U.S. Government agreed to appropriate reprisal action against North Vietnam.
>
> ...Today's joint response was carefully limited to military areas which are supplying men for attack in South Vietnam. As in the case of the North Vietnam attacks in the Gulf of Tonkin last August, the response is appropriate and fitting ..." Cmd. 2756, Vietnam No. 3, p. 10 (1965).

As will be noted, there is no allegation that the attackers included North Vietnamese.

83.

> These measures of self-help, which included war itself, were and are unsatisfactory. They may be used in the cause of justice ...but they may equally well be used for selfish purposes [quoting Hyde] ...When all is said and done, self-help is merely the exercise of might, which may not be also right. (CLYDE EAGLETON, INTERNATIONAL GOVERNMENT, 49-50, 3rd ed. 1957.) See also, e.g. 2 OPPENHEIM-LAUTERPACHT *op. cit. supra* note 54; at 43:
>
> Before the acceptance of the obligations of the Covenant of the League of Nations and of the Charter of the United Nations, States were entitled to have recourse to reprisal for such international delinquencies as they thought not important enough for a declaration of war, but too important to be entirely overlooked. That reprisals were a rough means for the settlement of disputes, and that the institution of reprisals would give, and had in the past given, occasion for abuse in case of a difference between a powerful and a weak State could not be denied.

84. CHARLES FENWICK, INTERNATIONAL LAW (4th ed., 1965), 637. Implying that military reprisals are a matter of the past, Professor Fenwick points out that "the more drastic reprisals were undistinguishable from war."

85. ROSALYN HIGGINS, THE DEVELOPMENT OF INTERNATIONAL LAW THROUGH THE POLITICAL ORGANS OF THE UNITED NATIONS 217 (1963), quoting Waldock, Jessup, Bowett, Stone, Wehberg and Schwarzenberger.

Many other authorities could be added; see, for example, the Belgian CHARLES DE VISSCHER, THEORY AND REALITY IN PUBLIC INTERNATIONAL LAW 288 (1957) ("resort to armed reprisals was a matter of pure political opportunism ...The States resorting to them were those powerful enough not to have to fear a riposte that might lead to war" [against *them*].) and the Australian J.G. STARKE, INTRODUCTION TO INTERNATIONAL LAW 390 (1963); and among still others quoted by the Memorandum, e.g. the Swiss jurist PAUL GUGGENHEIM, *II TRAITE DE*

DROIT INTERNATIONAL PUBLIC 86, 91 (1954): reprisals must not consist of acts "which constitute acts of war (*qui constituent des actes de guerre*)" and, in view of Article 2(4) of the Charter, "armed reprisal measures are inadmissible as much as is war (*les mesures de répresailles armeés sont donc inadmissible au même titre que la guerre*)" because "in the Charter ...it is not only war which is forbidden but the use of force in general (*dans la Charte ...ce n'est seulement la guerre qui est interdite, c'est l'emploi de la force en général*)."

Similarly, 2 OPPENHEIM-LAUTERPACHT at 152 declares: "The Charter seems to leave no room for doubt on the subject" and refutes at 154 the claim that North Vietnam's territorial integrity and political independence are not violated by U.S. war actions against it:

> Territorial integrity ...is synonymous with territorial inviolability. Thus a State would be acting in breach of its obligations under the Charter if it were to ...commit an act of force within the territory of another State ...to obtain redress, [even] without the intention of interfering permanently with the territorial integrity of that State.

86. For example, Resolutions S/5111, April 9, 1962; S/3538, Jan. 19, 1956; S/3139/Rev. 2, Nov. 24, 1953; S.C.O.R., 3rd yr., 354th mtg., at 39 ff.; see also Secretary General's Legal Opinion pursuant to S/3596 of April 4, 1956, quoted by HIGGINS, *op. cit. supra*, note 85, at 217-18.

87. Pursuant to Yemen's complaint to the Security Council, the British bombing raid on Harib in Yemen territory on March 28, 1964, preceded by the dropping of warning leaflets, caused death to 25 persons and injuries to scores of others (S/5673, par. 15), which figures were disputed by the United Kingdom.

In the extended debate in the Security Council (April 2 to 9, 1964), no speaker declared military reprisals to be permissible. Mr. Stevenson stated:

> My government has repeatedly expressed its emphatic disapproval of provocative acts and retaliatory raids, wherever they occur and by whomever they are committed. (S.C.O.R., 1108th mtg., Apr. 6, 1964, par. 67.)

It was pointed out that the United Kingdom had previously condemned military retaliation. With reference to an Israeli retaliation raid on the Syrian side of Lake Tiberias in the night of 11/12 December 1955 that according to the Syrian complaint (S/3525) caused 37 military and 12 civilian deaths and injuries to 5 soldiers, Sir Pierson Dixon declared in the Security Council, on January 12, 1956, eight years prior to the Yemen incident:

> We are strongly opposed ...to the whole idea that armed attack is in any way justified as retaliation for acts of hostility in the past, real or alleged ...It is true that on many occasions there has been provocation. It is also true that Israel has other legitimate complaints ...[But] whatever may have been the provocations

> in this case or as result of past incidents ...there can be no justification for retaliation which is all the more shocking when on the scale of the attack of [that] night ...Such retaliatory action is totally unjustified and ...a flagrant violation of ...the Charter. (S.C.O.R., 710th mtg., Jan. 12, 1956, par. 20, 30, 35; see also analogous statement by Sir Patrick Dean on behalf of the United Kingdom, S.C.O.R., 1003rd mtg., April 5, 1962, par. 31,32.)

Concerning the British raid on Harib on March 28, 1964, Sir Patrick Dean argued in the Security Council, departing from the original British explanation, that the bombing did not constitute retaliation or reprisal but was in defense of the South Arab Federation against repeated Yemenite raids, and was requested by the South Arab Federation. (S.C.O.R., 1109th mtg., Apr. 7, 1964, par. 25,26.) This explanation was not accepted by the Security Council. The Syrian delegate asserted that even if there had been armed attack by Yemen, the United Kingdom was not entitled to use force in defense under Article 51 of the Charter, because the South Arab Federation was not a Member of the United Nations. (S.C.O.R., 1109th mtg., April 7, 1964, par. 75-81.)

Eventually, the Security Council adopted a Resolution (188 of April 9, 1964) which, "Recalling Article 2, paragraphs 3 and 4 of the Charter of the United Nations,"

> 1. *Condemns* reprisals as incompatible with the purposes and principles of the United Nations;
> 2. *Deplores* the British military raids at Harib on 28 March 1964; and
> 3. *Deplores* all attacks and incidents which have occurred in the area.

The Resolution was carried by a vote of 9 to 0, with 2 abstentions (U.K. and U.S.A.). Ambassador Stevenson explained that the United States was unable to vote in favor of the Resolution because United States amendments which would have rephrased paragraphs 1ó3 in the following two paragraphs, were not accepted;

> *Condemns* both attacks and reprisals as incompatible with the purposes and principles of the United Nations.
>
> *Deplores* the British military action at Harib on 28 March 1964 and all attacks and incidents which have occurred in the area. (S.C.O.R., 1111th mtg., Apr. 9, 1964, par. 6.)

The representative of China, Mr. Liu Chieh, declared:

> In the course of the debate in the Council, it has been generally felt that the military action on the part of the British authorities constitutes a resort to force and, as such, is to be deplored. My delegation too finds it difficult to reconcile the use of force, even in the face of provocation, with the provisions of the United Nations Charter ...(*Ibid.*)

The Bolivian representative, Mr. Castrillo Justiniano, stated:

> Bolivia is compelled to align itself unreservedly with all the weak and defenseless countries which find themselves in a position similar to that of the small Arab Republic of Yemen. (*Ibid.*, par. 18.)

88. *Corfu Channel* Case (United Kingdom vs. Albania), Judgment of April 9, 1949, *I.C.J.* Reports 34-35 (1949).

89. Regarding the need for "closest scrutiny" of the illegality of the preceding act, see, *e.g.*, 1 GEORG SCHWARZENBERGER, INTERNATIONAL LAW 262 (2d ed., 1949).

90. *Newsweek*, Feb. 22, 1965, p. 11, described the development as follows: "two audacious Viet Cong raids on U.S. military bases brought a quick response when the U.S. chose to escalate the war by bombing and strafing strategic positions in North Vietnam."

91. The German-Portuguese Tribunal therefore judged as illegal the destruction, in 1914, by German troops of several Portuguese forts and frontier posts in reprisal for the killing of three German officials by a Portuguese frontier post at Naulilaa. 8 *Receuil M.A.T.*, at 409 (1929).

Georg Schwarzenberger (*op. cit. supra* note 89, at 262) also approves the decision of another Mixed Tribunal which "brushed aside" a claim of justified reprisal when it found that the party claiming violation of a treaty by the other party had itself "not the intention of carrying out" its own obligations under the treaty. 7 *Receuil M.A.T.*, at 865 (1928). See also, e.g., Louis B. Sohn: " ...a response should fit the violation. There should be some proportionality between the response and the violation." Sohn, *Response to Violations*, SECURITY IN DISARMAMENT 179 (Richard J. Barnet & Richard A. Falk, ed., 1965).

92. Characterization of the first bombings as proportionate reprisal may also have been dictated by the desire to prevent counterintervention by China. President Johnson emphasized in 1964 the possibility of such counterintervention in certain pre-election statements:

> [Aug. 13, 1964] Some ...ask us to take reckless action which might risk the lives of millions and engulf much of Asia and certainly threaten the peace of the entire world ...
>
> [Sept. 28, 1964] Some of our people—Mr. Nixon, Mr. Rockefeller, Mr. Scranton, and Mr. Goldwater—have all, at some time or other, suggested the possible wisdom of going north in Vietnam. Well, now, before you start attacking someone and launch a big offensive, you better give some consideration to how you are going to protect what you have ...I want to be very cautious and careful, and use it only as a last resort, when I start dropping bombs around that are likely to involve American boys in a war in Asia with 700 million Chinese ...So we are not going north ...
>
> [Oct. 1, 1964] it could have been easy in one wave to wipe out women and children and to drop bombs on North Vietnam and on China ...

> [Oct. 21, 1964] ...we have a choice. We can seek a wider war. China is there on the border with 700 million men, with over 300 million in their Army. And we could get tied down in a land war in Asia very quickly if we sought to throw our weight around ...

(quoted from David Wise, "Johnson's Own Words Trace Escalation," *New York Herald Tribune*, March 20, 1966, p. 14.)

93. See, *e.g.* Max Frankel, *New York Times*, March 3, 1966:

> ...U.S. forces in South Vietnam receive more than a thousand times the amount of supplies needed by theViet Cong ...The enemy has been fighting in the last year with an average daily flow of 12-30 tons of supplies from North Vietnam. But with somewhat larger shipments at present it is thought that the U.S. is moving an average of 24,600 tons of supplies each day by ship alone plus an undisclosed amount by air. The figures were made available by Secretary of Defense McNamara.
>
> ...Advocates of a longer bombing pause than the 37-day suspension that ended Jan. 31 [1966], contended that the military value of the bombing is minimal in view of the small amounts of supplies required by theViet Cong...

94. On February 13, 1965, a majority (Indian-Polish) Special Report of the ICC advised the co-Chairmen of the Geneva Conference that the military actions against the north on February 7 and again on February 8, 1965 (as reported to the ICC by the United States, South Vietnam and North Vietnam) "indicated violations of the Geneva Agreement." Reproduced in 1966 HEARINGS 730.

95. The Institute of International Law resolved in 1934 that "reprisals involving armed force are prohibited with the exception of action taken in self-defense [no reference to 'collective' self-defense] or in pursuance of properly authorized international action." Quoted in 2 OPPENHEIM-LAUTERPACHT 144, n. 1.

96. SIR H. WALDOCK, "The Regulation of the Use of Force by Individual States in International Law," 81 *Hague Receuil* 463 (1952).

97. Quoted by WILLIAM BISHOP, INTERNATIONAL LAW 778 (1962). —The Assembly of the League of Nations approved this Report, stating that Japan's action (invasion of China) was not justified under the right of self-defense, and in violation of certain treaties. OFF. J., SPEC. SUPPL. 177, p. 42; quoted in 2 OPPENHEIM-LAUTERPACHT, 152, n. 1.

98. Report of December 1, 1926. The statement is often approvingly quoted, e.g., by JESSUP, *op. cit. supra* 15, and by BOWETT, *op. cit. supra* note 15, at 238, who comments: "This applies with equal force to third states claiming the right to intervene by virtue of the concept of 'collective self-defense.'"

99. *New York Times*, April 21, 1966, p. 1.

100. FIELD MANUAL No. 27-10, issued by the Department of the Army, 3-4 (July 18, 1956).

The Manual cites various international Conventions to which the United States is a party, including: The Hague Regulations respecting the Laws and Customs of War on Land (annexed to Hague Convention No. IV of 1907, 36 Stat. 2277; Treaty Series 539); The Geneva Convention Relative to the Treatment of Prisoners of War of 1929 (47 Stat. 2021, T.S. 846); and the four Geneva Conventions of 1949, namely, "for the Amelioration of the Condition of the Wounded and Sick in Armed Forces in the Field" (T.I.A.S. 3362); "for the Ameloriation of the Condition of the Wounded, Sick and Shipwrecked Members of Armed Forces at Sea" (T.I.A.S. 3363); "relative to the Treatment of Prisoners of War"(T.I.A.S. 3364); and "relative to the Protection of Civilian Persons in Time of War" (T.I.A.S. 3365).

101. *Id.* at 4-5.

102. Sec. I, G, Memorandum of March 4, 1966: "a formal declaration of war would not place any obligation on either side in the conflict by which that side would not be bound in any event. The rules of international law concerning the conduct of hostilities in an international armed conflict apply regardless of any declaration of war."

Since the Memorandum insists that the war also in South Vietnam is an "international armed conflict," fought by theViet Cong as proxy for North Vietnam, this implies that the obligations apply also toward those belligerents.

However, the U.S. is under the same obligations pursuant to the legal position taken in the present Analysis, namely, that the conflict in South Vietnam is a civil strife. This character of the conflict only impinges on the legality of U.S. intervention; but it is evident that insofar as an outside State intervenes in a civil strife, such State is conducting international (and not civil) war. It is impossible to assert that the United States is conducting a civil war in Vietnam! Hence, although the South Vietnamese conflict is a civil war, the U.S. is still bound by the rules for international armed conflicts.

103. For text see WAR DEPT. TECHNICAL MANUAL TM27-251. *Treaties Governing Land Warfare* (1944).

104. There is reason for increasing concern that the United States is sometimes using the territory and people of Vietnam to experiment with new American weapons. See, *e.g.*, HANSON W. BALDWIN, "Vietnam is a Proving Ground for New Weapons," *New York Times*, May 1, 1966.

105. FIELD MANUAL No. 27-10, issued by the Department of the Army on July 18, 1956.

106. Statement of Feb. 4, 1966, quoted in Senate Foreign Relations Committee Hearings, THE TRUTH ABOUT VIETNAM, With an analysis

by Senator Wayne Morse and Foreword by Senator J.W. Fulbright, (1966) p. 95-96.

107. Senator Morse continued:

> ...the Defense Department estimates some 11,000 North Vietnamese troops are present in South Vietnam, whereas 215,000 U.S. troops are present ...North Vietnamese, or no North Vietnamese, it is the U.S. forces that are holding up General Ky. All the northerners could go home tomorrow, and Ky would still fail if the Americans did not remain. That is the evidence of the State Department figures. *Id.* at 10.

108. Jean Lacouture, the distinguished French writer who has been in Vietnam repeatedly since he first went there as a member of the staff of General Le Clerc in 1942, has written:

> American diplomacy is the victim of its own myths ...Notwithstanding the fact that the southern origin of theViet Cong insurrection has been fully confirmed, no element of the Vietnam problem has been so neglected, especially in American official circles. Lacouture, "Vietnam: The Lesson of War," *New York Review of Books*, March 3, 1966; republished in 1966 HEARINGS at 661-62.

109. A previous request by 28 members of the House of Representatives for public hearings by the House Foreign Affairs Committee was unsuccessful. See Hon. ROBERT W, KASTENMEIER, VIETNAM HEARINGS: VOICES FROM THE GRASSROOTS, Introduction (1965). Thereupon, Congressman Kastenmeier organized public hearings on July 30 and 31, 1965 in the Second Congressional District in Madison, Wisconsin.

110. The statements are quoted from Report on the U.S. Senate Hearings, THE TRUTH ABOUT VIETNAM, 5 *op. cit. supra*, note 106, p. 42.

Although these Hearings did not concentrate on legal questions, many statements of fact and law supporting the arguments submitted in the present analysis were made during them which, for lack of space, cannot be quoted here. That the conflict is a civil war has been pointed out from the floor of the United States Senate on other occasions, *e.g.*, by Senator Stephen M. Young, CONG. REC. 8454-55 (April 25, 1966).

111. THE TRUTH ABOUT VIETNAM, at 51-52.

112. *Id.* at 220.

113. *Id.* at 355.

114. *Id.* at 384.

115. *Id.* at 395.

116. With particular reference to treaties, including, *e.g.*, the United Nations Charter, Leo Gross emphasized "the venerable principles that an 'absurd' meaning should not be attributed to a treaty provision, that every provision should be interpreted in the context in which it appears, and that

the major purpose should be effectuated." Problems of ...Compliance with International Law," 59 AM. J. INT'L L. 55 (Jan. 1965); see also *passim*.

117. For example, Louis Henkin examines whether Communist subversion justifies military intervention: "The Powers determined to contain Communist expansion have aided non-Communist governments ...to win civil wars [as in Vietnam] ...The question ...is whether in the U.N. Charter ...there is law ...to deal with these situations." Henkin thereupon discusses persuasively the reasons militating against the interpretation of Articles 2(2) and 51 of the Charter as permitting force against Communist subversion as if it were an armed attack. The "absolute" prohibition of force, "the heart of the Charter," has, he insists, "the only exception" of self-defense against armed attack. Henkin, "Force, Intervention and Neutrality," 1963 *Proc. American Society of International Law* 155-59, 165-66; and passim.

118. Regarding the duty of non-intervention, Charles Fenwick pointed out: "The Charter of the United Nations ...clearly condemns the traditional forms of intervention as measures of self-help. Even the collective intervention of the United Nations as a body is prohibited in matters which are essentially within the domestic jurisdiction of any state, exception being made of enforcement measures taken by the Security Council ...[Q]uite clearly, the intervention by the Soviet Union in Hungary in 1956 was an outright violation of the prohibition. The intervention of the Soviet Union in Cuba in 1962, with the consent of Cuba, poses a separate issue, as does the intervention of the United States in Vietnam in 1965." FENWICK, *op. cit. supra* note 84, at 291.

119. CONG. REC. of March 15, 1966.

120. Arthur Krock, "The Sudden Rediscovery of SEATO," *New York Times*, March 6, 1966.

121.

Article 1: The Parties undertake, as set forth in the Charter of the United Nations, to settle any international disputes in which they may be involved by peaceful means in such a matter that international peace and security and justice are not endangered, and to refrain in their international relations from the threat or use of force in any manner inconsistent with the purposes of the United Nations.

Article 6, first sentence: This Treaty does not affect and shall not be interpreted as affecting in any way the rights and obligations of any of the Parties under the Charter of the United Nations ...

122.

Article 6, second sentence: Each Party declares that none of the international engagements now in force between it and any other of the Parties or any third Party is in conflict with the provisions of this Treaty ...

123. This formulation in the Protocol of September 8, 1954 to the SEATO Treaty acknowledges that only part of Vietnam ("the free territory")

is under the jurisdiction of the Diem regime, but does not disallow—and perhaps alludes to—the claim of the Diem regime for jurisdiction over South and North Vietnam.

124. "Differences [between NATO and SEATO] outnumber similarities ...the latter does not contain any equivalent of the NATO acknowledgement that an attack on a member [and Vietnam is not a SEATO member] is an attack on all." (RUTH C. LAWSON, ed., INTERNATIONAL REGIONAL ORGANIZATIONS 276 (1962).) Professor Lawson continues: "Also missing [in SEATO, as distinguished from NATO] is mention of armed force as possible means of resisting attack."

125.

> Article 2: ...the Parties ...will maintain and develop individual and collective capacities to resist armed attack and to prevent and counter subversive activities directed from without against their territorial integrity and political stability.

126. In fact, Secretary of State John Foster Dulles, main architect of SEATO, warned against such interpretation in connection with the so-called Eisenhower Doctrine which, under specific restrictions, authorized the President to use armed force to assist nations "in the general area of the Middle East" "against armed aggression from any country controlled by international communism":

> ...if you open the door to saying that any country which feels it is being threatened by subversive activities in another country is free to use armed force against that country, you are opening the door to a series of wars over the world, and I am confident that it would lead to a third world war. *The President's Proposal on the Middle East. Hearings before the Senate Committee on Foreign Relations* ...pt. I, p. 28 (1957).

127. *New York Times*, May 25, 1966, p. 7.

128. Press Release 166, reproduced in STATE DEP'T BULL. No. 1297, 692 (May 4, 1964).

129. As Mr. Rusk's summary shows, in April 1964 the SEATO Ministers merely authorized the members "to remain prepared" for "further steps," but did not authorize specific measures ("agree on the measures which should be taken," in the words of Article 4(2) SEATO). Such agreement was, however, an unconditional prerequisite for specific collective measures in a situation "other than ...armed attack."

130. "Our basic trouble in Vietnam is that we have not been proceeding under the [SEATO] treaty but going it alone ...we thought it was a minor concern we could handle ourselves without difficulty." KROCK, *op. cit. supra* note 120.

131. This principle was first agreed upon between the United States and Britain at the big-power Dumbarton Oaks Conference, Washington, 1944, which laid the groundwork for the subsequent multi-nation San

Francisco Conference. The two Powers agreed and the Soviet Union assented that "the Security Council was ...to use [regional] agencies 'where appropriate' for enforcement action under authority [of the Security Council]. But such agencies were not to take enforcement action without Security Council authorization." RUSSELL, *op. cit. supra* note 19, at 473.

This was also emphasized by Secretary of State Edward R. Stettinius in his statement of May 15, 1945: "the paramount authority of the world organization [the United Nations] in all enforcement action ...is already dealt with by the provision of the Dumbarton Oaks Proposals ...that no enforcement action will be taken by regional agencies without the authorization of the Security Council. It is not proposed to change this language" in the final text of the U.N. Charter which was then being discussed.

The international literature has also pointed out that it follows from the structure of the United Nations, that the Security Council can authorize regional enforcement only at the request of the regional organization. (See, *e.g.*, R. Monaco, *"La Fase Attuale del Regionalismo Internazionale"* in *CONTRIBUTI ALLO STUDIO DELLA ORGANIZZAZIONE INTERNAZIONALE* (Padova, 1957) pp. 204-05, quoting *UNCIO Selected Documents*, Washington, 189-99 (1946).)

132. According to the letter and spirit of the Charter, even "enforcement action" ordered by the Security Council should, whenever possible, consist of nonmilitary measures, such as stoppage of trade (economic sanctions) or severance of diplomatic relations (diplomatic sanctions), etc.

The original United States position as shown, *e.g.*, in its two draft plans for the United Nations (Dumbarton Oaks proposals) and in its proposals for the Rio Pact 1947, was that prior Security Council authorization is required also for nonmilitary enforcement actions to be taken under regional arrangements. By 1960, the United States claimed that regional enforcement actions not involving the use of force by the Organization of American States (O.A.S.) need only be reported to, but did not need prior authorization from the United Nations Security Council.

At that time, eight of the ten other Security Council members "either denied or expressed skepticism concerning the United States position ...that the authorization of the Security Council is not required for OAS sanctions short of military force." Inis L. Claude, Jr., "The O.A.S., the U.N. and the United States," *International Conciliation* 50, Carnegie Endowment for International Peace, No. 547 (March 1964). The United States has, however, never claimed that "enforcement" involving actual combat, as in Vietnam, is permissible under regional arrangements without previous United Nations Security Council authorization.

133. The State Department appears to deny this obligation by arguing (Sec. I. E) that it refers only to "relations among members of a regional arrangement," and that the Vietnam dispute is not a "local dispute" under

the South East Asia Treaty. The argument is most extraordinary. It seeks support from South Vietnam's inability, under the Geneva Accords, to join any alliance (which inability was circumvented by the "umbrella" device) and claims that this inability (designed to assure pacific settlement of the Vietnam problem) prevents efforts at pacific settlement. There is nothing in the history or wording of Article 52(2) to show that a "local dispute" may not involve nonmembers of the respective regional arrangement.

134. Regarding this and other points raised in the present Analysis, see also, *e.g.*, Henry Steel Commager, "Our Vietnamese Commitment," *Diplomat*, June 1966, pp. 23 ff.

135. *Op. cit. supra* note 105, at 49.

136. *Newsweek*, February 4, 1966, p. 19.

137. On Feb. 18, 1966, at the last session of the Hearings on Vietnam before the Senate Foreign Relations Committee, Chairman Senator Fulbright declared:

> ...unless we just assume that the world has gone completely mad ...[there should be a conference] including both Hanoi andViet Cong ...the Russians and the Chinese—everyone who has a legitimate interest ...you can[not] have a conference ...unless you ...give them some assurance that we mean what we say ...our actions are not consistent with our words ...I get the impression ...that we are in an unlimited war and the only kind of settlement [acceptable to the U.S.] is unconditional surrender ...that they come to the conference at your mercy and we have total victory. I see no occasion of any [U.S.] disposition to compromise ...I do not think you will get [a conference] until you propose reasonable terms ... 1966 HEARINGS at 387-92.

In mid-June 1966, Majority Leader Senator Mike Mansfield said:

> "With respect to Vietnam, we have scarcely begun to delineate the path to peace. We have yet ...to begin to devise a formula for the resolution of the conflict." Quoted by James Reston, *New York Times*, June 17, 1966, p. 44. Mr. Reston commented: "The Administration ...still believes ...that it can hurt the enemy enough to compel negotiations on Washington's terms."

138. "The majority of member states is increasingly concerned ...They are convinced that military methods will not restore peace in Vietnam ..." From address by Secretary General U Thant to the Amalgamated Clothing Workers of America, May 24, 1966, *New York Times*, May 25, 1966.

139. From address of May 24, 1966. On Feb. 12, 1965, after the war's escalation into North Vietnam, U Thant "most earnestly" insisted, as "many times before," that "only political and diplomatic methods ...may find a peaceful solution." On Feb. 24, 1965, he repeated that "the prospects for a peaceful settlement will be more and more remote as ...the aggravation [escalation] develops ...Of course, I have never advocated the immediate withdrawal of U.S. troops ...But ...once ...an agreed formula is at hand, if some sort of stability can be restored ...then, at that time, of course, the

U.S. can withdraw its troops with dignity." *U.N. Weekly Newsletters*, Feb. 19 and March 5, 1965.

140. At the Senate Foreign Relations Committee Hearings on Feb. 10, 1966, Mr. George Kennan stated: A "pall of discouragement has been cast" over the United Nations, because " a great many people at the U.N. saw the possibilities for peace rapidly deteriorating as this conflict in Vietnam became more intensive, and had a great deal of helplessness about it, because, after all, it was to have been the principal function of the U.N. organization to be able to prevent precisely this sort of a deterioration of the international atmosphere." *Op. cit. supra* note 106, at 196.

141. BOWETT, *op. cit. supra* notc 15, at 246.

142. Bowett also points out that even in the case of a sudden, real armed attack requiring immediate repulsion, there is no "general right of intervention [by third countries] at this stage: states not individually in a state of self-defense would have no right to take action or join in collective action. To allow them to do so would, at this stage, completely nullify the whole system of ...[the Charter] and signal a return to the very anarchy which the [United Nations] system ...is designed to prevent. The right of states that are not acting in [their own] self-defense to intervene must await the authorization of the competent organ of the centralized machinery, and this obligation cannot be avoided by a perversion of the concept of collective self-defense." *Id.* at 247.

See also, *e.g.*, Henkin, *op. cit. supra* note V 117, at 148-49.

143. The sudden reference in the State Department Memorandum to the whole of "Southeast Asia" is ominous; it may be intended to lay the groundwork for United States military intervention in other parts of the subcontinent. This interpretation is strengthened by the unprecedented scope of the Joint Resolution of Congress of August 10, 1964 (Gulf of Tonkin Resolution). For, as the Memorandum underscores (Sec. IV, C) the Joint Resolution "approved [for the future] the taking of 'all necessary measures ...to prevent further aggression'"—without limitation of the countries whose aggression the United States may prevent by military action.

As also quoted by the Memorandum, Senator Morse described the resolution as a "pre-dated declaration of war." It can, indeed, be construed as an indirect, pre-dated declaration of preventive war against an undetermined number of countries.

144. Hans Kelsen, one of the authorities relied on by the Memorandum, stated that the United States could not have invoked the right of collective self-defense; and that, in fact, since only the subsequent Council Resolution of June 27, 1951 justified armed sanctions, U.S. armed intervention prior to that second Resolution was not justified. KELSEN, THE LAW OF NATIONS (Supp. at 931).

Kelsen also points out that since the Security Council Resolutions referred to "authorities of Northern Korea" in contradistinction to the "Government of the Republic of Korea," the Korean conflict can be considered as civil war. *Id.* at 928 ff. Since the Council has the right to intervene when it determines the existence of breach of the peace in whatever situation, the Council (but no individual state) was entitled to intervene, regardless of whether the situation was a civil war or not.

145. The insistence on peaceful settlements of disputes is also stated in other Articles of the United Nations Charter, for example, Article 52(2), and in fact permeates the whole Charter, as shown in its opening words, "to save succeeding generations from the scourge of war." It is expressed in numerous Resolutions of United Nations organs adopted with the vote of the United States.

146. Senator ERNEST GRUENING, "The Reality of Vietnam," *The Progressive*, April 1966, p. 16:

> We should have invoked the offices of the United Nation at the beginning, when we felt that treaty commitments were violated. We have not used the United Nations as we should have.

The Senator's constructive suggestion is:

> What the United States should do—in sum—is to return to the rule of law.

147. Senator VANCE HARTKE, "Where are the Peacemakers?" *The Progressive*, Sept. 1966, pp. 12-14. *Cfr.* also FRANZ SCHUMANN *et al.*, THE POLITICS OF ESCALATION IN VIETNAM, foreword by Arthur Schlesinger, Jr. (1966).

148. As long ago as 1950, the General Assembly agreed in the Resolution on the Duties of States in the Case of Outbreak of Hostilities that states engaged in hostilities "take all steps practicable in the circumstances ...to bring the armed conflict to an end at the earliest possible moment." Res. 378 (V).

149. C.F.SALANS, "The International Conference on the Settlement of the Laotian Question and the Geneva Agreements of 1962," 57 AM. J. INT'L L., April, 1963, pp. 301, 306-07. *Cfr.* also ANTHONY EDEN, TOWARD PEACE IN INDOCHINA (1966).

A Laos-type settlement for Vietnam has, for example, been urged by ARTHUR SCHLESINGER, Jr., *New York Times Magazine*, Sept. 18, 1966, p. 119: "It is hard to see why we should not follow the precedent of Laos." TheViet Cong [N.L.F.] should be admitted to the Vietnam peace talks, under the same conditions under which the Pathet Lao was admitted to the 1962 Laos peace talks. "Nor is there reason to see why we have been so reluctant again to follow the Laos model and declare neutralization, under international guarantee, our long-run objective for Vietnam. An imaginative diplomacy would long since have discussed the ways and means of such neutralization with ...interested countries. Unsatisfactory as the situation in Laos may be today, it is still incomparably better than the situation in South Vietnam."

150. DEPT. OF STATE BULL. XXXI, Nov. 15, 1954, pp. 735-36. The letter constitutes a "highly tentative, highly conditional opening of negotiations and statement of hopes." " ...the nearest thing to a commitment at this stage was an indicated willingness, subject to some stiff (and as yet unsatisfied) conditions and understanding, to provide economic and technical assistance, including military advisers, material, and training." DON R. and ARTHUR LARSON, VIETNAM AND BEYOND (1965); reprinted in part in Raskin & Fall, *op. cit. supra* note 49, at 99 ff.

151. Quoted by DON R. & ARTHUR LARSON, *Id.*, reprinted in Raskin & Fall, at 105.

152. HANSON W. BALDWIN, "U.S. in Vietnam Builds Up, and Up, and Up," *New York Times*, June 19, 1966, p. E-3: Since "March 1965, the Pentagon has developed a phased buildup of strength" for South Vietnam. "Phase I ...scheduled to be completed at the end of [1965] called for 210,000 troops in Vietnam." Whereas "the original Phase II ...contemplated about 350,000 troops in Vietnam about now [mid-June 1966], there were actually 267,000 there on June 11." By the end of 1966, "year-end planned strength [is to be] 350,000 to 400,000 men." But "the ultimate figure must remain in doubt." Mr. Baldwin refers to Senator Stennis' estimate of January 1966 that he (Senator Stennis) "would not be surprised if 'we were ultimately required to commit 600,000 men in the battle.'"

These figures include neither the United States naval forces in the area, nor any United States forces participating in the war but stationed outside of South Vietnam.

153. The high respect for international law that characterizes the Constitution is expressed in Article I, Section 8(10), specifically granting Congress the power "to define and punish ...offenses against the law of nations." This provision envisages, far ahead of its time, Congressional statutes that would make individuals punishable for offenses against the law of nations—that is, not only for offenses against ratified treaties but for offenses against customary international law. See also *The Paquete Habana* decision of the U.S. Supreme Court, 175 U.S. 677.

154. It may be stated that even in spite of that Security Council authorization, doubts have been expressed about the constitutional aspects, and are to be found in textbooks on constitutional law for college undergraduates. For example, JOHN H. FERGUSON & DEAN E. MCHENRY, THE AMERICAN SYSTEM OF GOVERNMENT, 312-13 (7th ed. 1963) wrote:

> President Truman's prompt action in ordering American forces to aid the South Koreans was challenged then and subsequently as exceeding his authority as

Commander in Chief. He ought, critics argued, to have consulted Congress and sought congressional approval ...A substantial body of opinion consistently supported the President's action as a valid exercise of his power to dispose and assign the armed forces ...In view of the speed with which the nation is likely to become involved in international crises [as shown above, such "speed" was absent in the Vietnam situation which, on the contrary, festered over many years], the President's plenary authority over the armed forces no doubt will prevail. Thoughtful citizens, however, fear future misuse of such near-absolute power ...

155. Mr. George Kennan, in his formal statement to the Senate Foreign Relations Committee in February 1966, presented "from the deepest and most troubled concern that we should find the ...right course, at this truly crucial moment," said:

> The first point I would like to make is that if we were not already involved as we are today in Vietnam, I would know of no reason why we should wish to become so involved, and I could think of several reasons why we should wish not to.

He warned against

> considerations of prestige that arise precisely out of our present involvement ...the spectacle ...of Americans inflicting grievous injury on ...a poor and helpless people ...of different race and color ...produces reactions ...throughout the world profoundly detrimental to the image we would like them to hold of this country ...A victory purchased at the price of further such damage would be a hollow one in terms of our world interests ... See *op. cit. supra* note 105, at 190-92.

Appendix I

The Legality of United States Participation in the Defense of Vietnam

Memorandum from the Department of State, Office of the Legal Adviser, March 4, 1966

(*Congressional Record*, Vol. 112, No. 43, of March 10, 1966, pp. 5274-5279)

This legal memorandum was prepared by Leonard C. Meeker, Legal Adviser of the Department and was submitted to the Senate Committee on Foreign Relations on March 8, 1966.

I. The United States and South Vietnam Have the Right under International Law to Participate in the Collective Defense of South Vietnam against Armed Attack.

In response to requests from the Government of South Vietnam, the United States has been assisting that country in defending itself against armed attack from the Communist North. This attack has taken the forms of externally supported subversion, clandestine supply of arms, infiltration of armed personnel, and most recently the sending of regular units of the North Vietnamese army into the South.

International law has long recognized the right of individual and collective self-defense against armed attack. South Vietnam and the United States are engaging in such collective defense consistently with international law and with United States obligations under the United Nations Charter.

A. South Vietnam is Being Subjected to Armed Attack by Communist North Vietnam.

The Geneva Accords of 1954 established a demarcation line between North Vietnam and South Vietnam. They provided for withdrawals of military forces into the respective zones north and south of this line. The Accords prohibited the use of either zone for the resumption of hostilities or to "further an aggressive policy."

During the 5 years following the Geneva Conference of 1954, the Hanoi regime developed a covert political-military organization in South Vietnam based on Communist cadres it had ordered to stay in the South, contrary to the provisions of the Geneva Accords. The activities of this covert organization were directed toward the kidnapping and assassination of civilian officials—acts of terrorism that were perpetrated in increasing numbers.

In the 3-year period from 1959 to 1961, the North Vietnam regime infiltrated an estimated 10,000 men into the South. It is estimated that 13,000 additional personnel were infiltrated in 1962, and, by the end of 1964, North Vietnam may well have moved over 40,000 armed and unarmed guerrillas into South Vietnam.

The International Control Commission reported in 1962 the findings of its Legal Committee:

> ...there is evidence to show that arms, armed and unarmed personnel, munitions and other supplies have been sent from the Zone in the North to the Zone in the South with the objective of supporting and carrying out hostile activities, including armed attacks, directed against the Armed Forces and Administration of the Zone in the South.
>
> ...there is evidence that the PAVN [People's Army of Vietnam] has allowed the Zone in the North to be used for inciting, encouraging and supporting hostile activities in the Zone in the South, aimed at the overthrow of the Administration in the South.

Beginning in 1964, the Communists apparently exhausted their reservoir of Southerners who had gone North. Since then the greater number of men infiltrated into the South have been native-born North Vietnamese. Most recently, Hanoi has begun to infiltrate elements of the North Vietnamese army in increasingly larger numbers. Today, there is evidence that nine regiments of regular North Vietnamese forces are fighting in organized units in the South.

In the guerrilla war in Vietnam, the external aggression from the North is the critical military element of the insurgency, although it is unacknowledged by North Vietnam. In these circumstances, an "armed attack" is not as easily fixed by date and hour as in the case of traditional warfare. However, the infiltration of thousands of armed men clearly constitutes an "armed attack" under any reasonable definition. There may be some question as to the exact date at which North Vietnam's aggression grew into an "armed attack," but there can be no doubt that it had occurred before February 1965.

B. International Law Recognizes the Right of Individual and Collective Self-Defense Against Armed Attack.

International law has traditionally recognized the right of self-defense against armed attack. This proposition has been asserted by writers on international law through the several centuries in which the modern law of nations has developed. The proposition has been acted on numerous times by governments throughout modern history. Today the principle of self-defense against armed attack is universally recognized and accepted.[1]

The Charter of the United Nations, concluded at the end of World War II, imposed an important limitation on the use of force by United Nations Members. Article 2, paragraph 4, provides:

> All Members shall refrain in their international relations from the threat or use of force against the territorial integrity or political independence of any state, or in any other manner inconsistent with the Purposes of the United Nations.

In addition, the Charter embodied a system of international peacekeeping through the organs of the United Nations. Article 24 summarizes these structural arrangements in stating that the United Nations Members:

> ...confer on the Security Council primary responsibility for the maintenance of international peace and security, and agree that in carrying out its duties under this responsibility the Security Council acts on their behalf.

However, the Charter expressly states in article 51 that the remaining provisions of the Charter—including the limitation of article 2, paragraph 4, and the creation of United Nations machinery to keep the peace—in no way diminish the right of self-defense against armed attack. Article 51 provides:

> Nothing in the present Charter shall impair the inherent right of individual or collective self-defense if an armed attack occurs against a Member of the United Nations, until the Security Council has taken the measures necessary to maintain international peace and security. Measures taken by Members in the exercise of this right of self-defense shall be immediately reported to the Security Council and shall not in any way affect the authority and responsibility of the Security Council under the present Charter to take at any time such action as it deems necessary in order to maintain or restore international peace and security.

Thus, article 51 restates and preserves, for Member states in the situations covered by the article, a long-recognized principle of international law. The article is a "saving clause" designed to make clear that no other provision in the Charter shall be interpreted to impair the inherent right of self-defense referred to in article 51.

Three principle objections have been raised against the availability of the right of individual and collective self-defense in the case of Vietnam: (1) that this right applies only in the case of an armed attack on a United Nations Member; (2) that it does not apply in the case of South Vietnam because the latter is not an independent sovereign state; and (3) that collective self-defense may be undertaken only by a regional organization operating under chapter VII of the United Nations Charter. These objections will now be considered in turn.

C. The Right of Individual and Collective Self-Defense Applies in the Case of South Vietnam Whether or Not That Country Is a Member of the United Nations.

1. South Vietnam enjoys the right of self-defense.

The argument that the right of self-defense is available only to Members of the United Nations mistakes the nature of the right of self-defense and the relationship of the United Nations Charter to international law in this respect. As already shown, the right of self-defense against armed attack is an inherent right under international law. The right is not conferred by the Charter, and, indeed, article 51 expressly recognizes that the right is inherent.

The Charter nowhere contains any provisions designed to deprive non-Members of the right of self-defense against armed attack.[2] Article 2, paragraph 6, does charge the United Nations with responsibility for insuring that non-Member states act in accordance with United Nations "Principles so far as may be necessary for the maintenance of international peace and security." Protection against aggression and self-defense against armed attack are important elements in the whole Charter scheme for the maintenance of international peace and security. To deprive nonMembers of their inherent right of self-defense would not accord with the principles of the organization, but would be prejudicial to the maintenance of peace. Thus article 2, paragraph 6—and, indeed, the rest of the Charter—should certainly not be construed to nullify or diminish the inherent defensive rights of non-Members.

2. The United States has the right to assist in the defense of South Vietnam although the latter is not a United Nations Member.

The cooperation of two or more international entities in the defense of one or both against armed attack is generally referred to as collective self-defense. United States participation in the defense of South Vietnam at the latter's request is an example of collective self-defense.

The United States is entitled to exercise the right of individual or collective self-defense against armed attack, as that right exists in international law, subject only to treaty limitations and obligations undertaken by this country.

It has been urged that the United States has no right to participate in the collective defense of South Vietnam because article 51 of the United Nations Charter speaks only of the situation "if an armed attack occurs *against a Member of the United Nations*." This argument is without substance.

In the first place, article 51 does not impose restrictions or cut down the otherwise available rights of United Nations Members. By its own terms, the article preserves an inherent right. It is, therefore, necessary to look elsewhere in the Charter for any obligation of Members restricting their participation in collective defense of an entity that is not a United Nations Member.

Article 2, paragraph 4, is the principal provision of the Charter imposing limitations on the use of force by Members. It states that they:

> ...shall refrain in their international relations from the threat or use of force against the territorial integrity or political independence of any state, or in any other manner inconsistent with the Purposes of the United Nations.

Action taken in defense against armed attack cannot be characterized as falling within this proscription. The record of the San Francisco Conference makes clear that article 2, paragraph 4, was not intended to restrict the right of self-defense against armed attack.[3]

One will search in vain for any other provision in the Charter that would preclude United States participation in the collective defense of a non-Member. The fact that article 51 refers only to armed attack "against a Member of the United Nations" implies no intention to preclude Members from participating in the defense of non-Members. Any such result would have seriously detrimental consequences for international peace and security and would be inconsistent with the purposes of the United Nations as they are set forth in article 1 of the Charter.[4] The right of Members to participate in the defense of non-Members is upheld by leading authorities on international law.[5]

D. The Right of Individual and Collective Self-Defense Applies Whether or Not South Vietnam Is Regarded as an Independent Sovereign State.

1. *South Vietnam enjoys the right of self-defense.*

It has been asserted that the conflict in Vietnam is "civil strife" in which foreign intervention is forbidden. Those who make this assertion have gone so far as to compare Ho Chi Minh's actions in Vietnam with the efforts of President Lincoln to preserve the Union during the American Civil War. Any such characterization is an entire fiction disregarding the actual situation in Vietnam. The Hanoi regime is anything but the legitimate government of a unified country in which the South is rebelling against lawful national authority.

The Geneva Accords of 1954 provided for a division of Vietnam into two zones at the 17th parallel. Although this line of demarcation was intended to be temporary, it was established by international agreement, which specifically forbade aggression by one zone against the other.

The Republic of Vietnam in the South has been recognized as a separate international entity by approximately 60 governments the world over. It has been admitted as a Member of a number of the specialized agencies of the United Nations. The United Nations General Assembly in 1957 voted to recommend South Vietnam for Membership in the organization, and its admission was frustrated only by the veto of the Soviet Union in the Security Council.

In any event there is no warrant for the suggestion that one zone of a temporarily divided state—whether it be Germany, Korea, or Vietnam—can be legally overrun by armed forces from the other zone, crossing the internationally recognized line of demarcation between the two. Any such doctrine would subvert the international agreement establishing the line of demarcation, and would pose grave dangers to international peace.

The action of the United Nations in the Korean conflict of 1950 clearly established that there is no greater license for one zone of a temporarily divided state to attack the other zone than there is for one state to attack another state. South Vietnam has the same right that South Korea had to defend itself and to organize collective defense against an armed attack from the North. A resolution of the Security Council dated June 25, 1950, noted "with grave concern the armed attack upon the Republic of Korea by forces from North Korea" and determined "that this action constitutes a breach of the peace.

2. The United States is entitled to participate in the collective defense of South Vietnam whether or not the latter is regarded as an independent sovereign state.

As stated earlier, South Vietnam has been recognized as a separate international entity by approximately 60 governments. It has been admitted to Membership in a number of the United Nations specialized agencies and has been excluded from the United Nations Organization only by the Soviet veto.

There is nothing in the Charter to suggest that United Nations Members are precluded from participating in the defense of a recognized international entity against armed attack merely because the entity may lack some of the attributes of an independent sovereign state. Any such result would have a destructive effect on the stability of international engagements such as the Geneva Accords of 1954 and on internationally agreed lines of demarcation. Such a result, far from being in accord with the Charter and the purposes of the United Nations, would undermine them and would create new dangers to international peace and security.

E. The United Nations Charter Does Not Limit the Right of Self-Defense to Regional Organizations.

Some have argued that collective self-defense may be undertaken only by a regional arrangement or agency operating under chapter VIII of the United Nations Charter. Such an assertion ignores the structure of the Charter and the practice followed in the more than 20 years since the founding of the United Nations.

The basic proposition that right of self-defense is not impaired by the Charter—as expressly stated in article 51—is not conditioned by any Charter provision limiting the application of this proposition to collective defense by a regional arrangement or agency. The structure of the Charter reinforces this conclusion. Article 51 appears in chapter VII of the Charter, entitled "Action With Respect to Threats to the Peace, Breaches of the Peace, and Acts of Aggression," whereas chapter VIII, entitled "Regional Arrangements," begins with article 52 and embraces the two following articles. The records of the San Francisco Conference show that article 51 was deliberately placed in chapter VII rather than chapter VIII, "where it would only have a bearing on the regional system."[6]

Under article 51, the right of self-defense is available against any armed attack, whether or not the country attacked is a member of a regional arrangement and regardless of the source of the attack. Chapter VIII, on the other hand, deals with relations among members of a regional arrangement or agency, and authorizes regional action as appropriate for dealing with "local disputes." This distinction has been recognized ever since the founding of the United Nations in 1945.

For example, the North Atlantic Treaty has operated as a collective security arrangement, designed to take common measures in preparation against the eventuality of an armed attack for which collective defense under article 51 would be required. Similarly, the Southeast Asia Treaty Organization was designed as a collective defense arrangement under article 51. Secretary of State Dulles emphasized this in his testimony before the Senate Foreign Relations Committee in 1954.

By contrast, article 1 of the Charter of Bogota (1948), establishing the Organization of American States, expressly declares that the organization is a regional agency within the United Nations. Indeed, chapter VIII of the United Nations Charter was included primarily to take account of the functioning of the inter-American system.

In sum, there is no basis in the United Nations Charter for contending that the right of self-defense against armed attack is limited to collective defense by a regional organization.

F. The United States Has Fulfilled Its Obligations to the United Nations.

A further argument has been made that the Members of the United Nations have conferred on United Nations organs—and, in particular, on the Security Council—exclusive power to act against armed aggression. Again, the express language of article 51 contradicts that assertion. A victim of armed attack is not required to forgo individual or collective defense of its territory until such time as the United Nations organizes collective action and takes appropriate measures. To the contrary, article 51 clearly states that the right of self-defense may be exercised "*until* the Security Council has taken the measures necessary to maintain international peace and security."[7]

As indicated earlier, article 51 is not literally applicable to the Vietnam situation since South Vietnam is not a Member. However, reasoning by analogy from article 51 and adopting its provisions as an appropriate guide for the conduct of Members in a case like Vietnam, one can only conclude that United States actions are fully in accord with this country's obligations as a Member of the United Nations.

Article 51 requires that:

> Measures taken by Members in the exercise of this right of self-defense shall be immediately reported to the Security Council and shall not in any way affect the authority and responsibility of the Security Council under the present Charter to take at any time such action as it deems necessary in order to maintain or restore international peace and security.

The United States has reported to the Security Council on measures it has taken in countering the Communist aggression in Vietnam. In August 1964 the United States asked the Council to consider the situation created by North Vietnamese attacks on United States destroyers in the Tonkin Gulf. The Council thereafter met to debate the question, but adopted no resolutions. Twice in February 1965 the United States sent additional reports to the Security Council on the conflict in Vietnam and on the additional measures taken by the United States in the collective defense of South Vietnam. In January 1966 the United States formally submitted the Vietnam question to the Security Council for its consideration and introduced a draft resolution calling for discussions looking toward a peaceful settlement on the basis of the Geneva Accords.

At no time has the Council taken any action to restore peace and security in Southeast Asia. The Council has not expressed criticism of United States actions. Indeed, since the United States submission of January 1966, Members of the Council have been notably reluctant to proceed with any consideration of the Vietnam question.

The conclusion is clear that the United States has in no way acted to interfere with United Nations consideration of the conflict in Vietnam. On the contrary, the United States has requested United Nations consideration, and the Council has not seen fit to act.

G. International Law Does Not Require a Declaration of War as a Condition Precedent To Taking Measures of Self-Defense against Armed Attack.

The existence or absence of a formal declaration of war is not a factor in determining whether an international use of force is lawful as a matter of international law. The United Nations Charter's restrictions focus on the manner and purpose of its use and not on any formalities of announcement.

It should also be noted that a formal declaration of war would not place any obligations on either side in the conflict by which that side would not be bound in any event. The rules of international law concerning the conduct of hostilities in an international armed conflict apply regardless of any declaration of war.

H. Summary

The analysis set forth above shows that South Vietnam has the right in present circumstances to defend itself against armed attack from the North and to organize a collective self-defense with the participation of others. In response to requests from South Vietnam, the United States has been participating in that defense, both through military action within South Vietnam and actions taken directly against the aggressor in North Vietnam. This participation by the United States is in conformity with international law and is consistent with our obligations under the Charter of the United Nations.

II. The United States Has Undertaken Commitments To Assist South Vietnam in Defending Itself against Communist Aggression from the North.

The United States has made commitments and given assurances, in various forms and at different times, to assist in the defense of South Vietnam.

A. The United States Gave Undertakings at the End of the Geneva Conference in 1954.

At the time of the signing of the Geneva Accords in 1954, President Eisenhower warned "that any renewal of Communist aggression would be viewed by us as a matter of grave concern," at the same time giving assurance that the United States would "not use force to disturb the settlement." And the formal declaration made by the United States Government at the conclusion of the Geneva Conference stated that the United States "would view any renewal of the aggression in violation of the aforesaid agreements with grave concern and as seriously threatening international peace and security."

B. The United States Undertook an International Obligation To Defend South Vietnam in the SEATO Treaty.

Later in 1954 the United States negotiated with a number of other countries and signed the Southeast Asia Collective Defense Treaty. The treaty contains in the first paragraph of article IV the following provision:

> Each Party recognizes that aggression by means of armed attack in the treaty area against any of the Parties or against any State or territory which the Parties by unanimous agreement may hereafter designate, would endanger its own peace and safety, and agrees that it will in that event act to meet the common danger in accordance with its constitutional processes. Measures taken under this paragraph shall be immediately reported to the Security Council of the United Nations.

Annexed to the treaty was a protocol stating that:

> The Parties to the Southeast Asia Collective Defense Treaty unanimously designate for the purposes of Article IV of the Treaty the States of Cambodia and Laos and the free territory under the jurisdiction of the State of Vietnam.

Thus, the obligations of article IV, paragraph 1, dealing with the eventuality of armed attack, have from the outset covered the territory of South Vietnam. The facts as to the North Vietnamese armed attack against the South have been summarized earlier, in the discussion of the right of self-defense under international law and the Charter of the United Nations. The term "armed attack" has the same meaning in the SEATO treaty as in the United Nations Charter.

Article IV, paragraph 1, places an obligation on each party to the SEATO treaty to "act to meet the common danger in accordance with its constitutional processes" in the event of an armed attack. The treaty does not require a collective determination that an armed attack has occurred in order that the obligation of article IV, paragraph 1, become operative. Nor does the provision require collective decision on actions to be taken to meet the common danger. As Secretary Dulles pointed out when transmitting the treaty to the President, the commitment in article IV, paragraph 1, "leaves to the judgment of each country the type of action to be taken in the event an armed attack occurs."

The treaty was intended to deter armed aggression in Southeast Asia. To that end it created not only a multilateral alliance but also a series of bilateral relationships. The obligations are placed squarely on "each Party" in the event of armed attack in the treaty area—not upon "the Parties," a wording that might have implied a necessity for collective decision. The treaty was intended to give the assurance of United States assistance to any party or protocol state that might suffer a Communist armed attack, regardless of the views or actions of other parties. The fact that the obligations are individual, and may even to some extent differ among the parties to the treaty, is demonstrated by the United States understanding, expressed at the time of signature, that its obligations under article IV, paragraph 1, apply only in the event of *Communist* aggression, whereas the other parties to the treaty were unwilling so to limit their obligations to each other.

Thus, the United States has a commitment under article IV, paragraph 1, in the event of armed attack, independent of the decision or action of other treaty parties. A joint statement issued by Secretary Rusk and Foreign Minister Thanat Khoman of Thailand on March 6, 1962, reflected this understanding:

> The Secretary of State assured the Foreign Minister that in the event of such aggression, the United States intends to give full effect to its obligations under the Treaty to act to meet the common danger in accordance with its constitutional processes. The Secretary of State reaffirmed that this obligation of the United States does not depend upon the prior agreement of all parties to the Treaty, since this Treaty obligation is individual as well as collective.

Most of the SEATO countries have stated that they agreed with this interpretation. None has registered objection to it.

When the Senate Committee on Foreign Relations reported on the Southeast Asia Collective Defense Treaty, it noted that the treaty area was further defined so that the "Free Territory of Vietnam" was an area "which, if attacked, would fall under the protection of the instrument." In its conclusion the committee stated:

> The committee is not impervious to the risks which this treaty entails. It fully appreciates that acceptance of these additional obligations commits the United States to a course of action over a vast expanse of the Pacific. Yet these risks are consistent with our own highest interests.

The Senate gave its advice and consent to the treaty by a vote of 82 to 1.

C. The United States Has Given Additional Assurances to the Government of South Vietnam.

The United States has also given a series of additional assurances to the Government of South Vietnam. As early as October 1954 President Eisenhower undertook to provide direct assistance to help make South

Vietnam "capable of resisting attempted subversion or aggression through military means." On May 11, 1957, President Eisenhower and President Ngo Dinh Diem of the Republic of Vietnam issued a joint statement which called attention to "the large build-up of Vietnamese Communist military forces in North Vietnam" and stated:

> Noting that the Republic of Vietnam is covered by Article IV of the Southeast Asia Collective Defense Treaty, President Eisenhower and President Ngo Dinh Diem agreed that aggression or subversion threatening the political independence of the Republic of Vietnam would be considered as endangering peace and stability.

On August 2, 1961, President Kennedy declared that "the United States is determined that the Republic of Vietnam shall not be lost to the Communists for lack of any support which the United States Government can render." On December 7 of that year President Diem appealed for additional support. In his reply of December 14, 1961, President Kennedy recalled the United States declaration made at the end of the Geneva Conference in 1954, and reaffirmed that the United States was "prepared to help the Republic of Vietnam to protect its people and to preserve its independence." This assurance has been reaffirmed many times since.

III. Actions by the United States and South Vietnam Are Justified under the Geneva Accords of 1954.

A. Description of the Accords

The Geneva Accords of 1954[8] established the date and hour for a cease-fire in Vietnam, drew a "provisional military demarcation line" with a demilitarized zone on both sides, and required an exchange of prisoners and the phased regroupment of Viet Minh forces from the south to the north and of French Union forces from the north to the south. The introduction into Vietnam of troop reinforcements and new military equipment (except for replacement and repair) was prohibited. The armed forces of each party were required to respect the demilitarized zone and the territory of the other zone. The adherence of either zone to any military alliance, and the use of either zone for the resumption of hostilities to "further an aggressive policy," were prohibited. The International Control Commission was established, composed of India, Canada and Poland, with India as chairman. The task of the Commission was to supervise the proper execution of the provisions of the cease-fire agreement. General elections that would result in reunification were required to be held in July 1956 under the supervision of the ICC.

B. North Vietnam Violated the Accords From the Beginning.

From the very beginning, the North Vietnamese violated the 1954 Geneva Accords. Communist military forces and supplies were left in the South in violation of the Accords. Other Communist guerrillas were moved north for further training and then were infiltrated into the South in violation of the Accords.

C. The Introduction of United States Military Personnel and Equipment Was Justified.

The Accords prohibited the reinforcement of foreign military forces in Vietnam and the introduction of new military equipment, but they allowed replacement of existing military personnel and equipment. Prior to late 1961 South Vietnam had received considerable military equipment and supplies from the United States, and the United States had gradually enlarged its Military Assistance Advisory Group to slightly less than 900 men. These actions were reported to the ICC and were justified as replacements for equipment in Vietnam in 1954 and for French training and advisory personnel who had been withdrawn after 1954.

As the Communist aggression intensified during 1961, with increased infiltration and a marked stepping up of Communist terrorism in the South, the United States found it necessary in late 1961 to increase substantially the numbers of our military personnel and the amounts and types of equipment introduced by this country into South Vietnam. These increases were justified by the international law principle that a material breach of an agreement by one party entitles the other at least to withhold compliance with an equivalent, corresponding, or related provision until the defaulting party is prepared to honor its obligations.[9]

In accordance with this principle, the systematic violation of the Geneva Accords by North Vietnam justified South Vietnam in suspending compliance with the provision controlling entry of foreign military personnel and military equipment.

D. South Vietnam Was Justified in Refusing To Implement the Election Provision of the Geneva Accords.

The Geneva Accords contemplated the reunification of the two parts of Vietnam. They contained a provision for general elections to be held in July 1956 in order to obtain a "free expression of the national will." The Accords stated that "consultations will be held on this subject between the competent representative authorities of the two zones from 20 July 1955 onwards."

There may be some question whether South Vietnam was bound by these election provisions. As indicated earlier, South Vietnam did not sign the cease-fire agreement of 1954, nor did it adhere to the Final Declaration of the Geneva Conference. The South Vietnamese Government at that time gave notice of its objection in particular to the election provisions of the Accords.

However, even on the premise that these provisions were binding on South Vietnam, the South Vietnamese Government's failure to engage in consultations in 1955, with a view to holding elections in 1956, involved no breach of obligation. The conditions in North Vietnam during that period were such as to make impossible any free and meaningful expression of popular will.

Some of the facts about conditions in the North were admitted even by the Communist leadership in Hanoi. General Giap, currently Defense Minister of North Vietnam, in addressing the Tenth Congress of the North Vietnamese Communist Party in October 1956, publicly acknowledged that the Communist leaders were running a police state where executions, terror, and torture were commonplace. A nationwide election in these circumstances would have been a travesty. No one in the North would have dared to vote except as directed. With a substantial majority of the Vietnamese people living north of the 17th parallel, such an election would have meant turning the country over to the Communists without regard to the will of the people. The South Vietnamese Government realized these facts and quite properly took the position that consultation for elections in 1956 as contemplated by the Accords would be a useless formality.[10]

IV. The President Has Full Authority To Commit United States Forces in the Collective Defense of South Vietnam.

There can be no question in present circumstances of the President's authority to commit United States forces to the defense of South Vietnam. The grant of authority to the President in article II of the Constitution extends to the actions of the United States currently undertaken in Vietnam. In fact, however, it is unnecessary to determine whether this grant standing alone is sufficient to authorize the actions taken in Vietnam. These actions rest not only on the exercise of Presidential powers under article II but on the SEATO treaty—a treaty advised and consented to by the Senate—and on actions of the Congress, particularly the joint resolution of August 10, 1964. When these sources of authority are taken together—article II of the Constitution, the SEATO treaty, and actions by the Congress—there can be no question of the legality under domestic law of United States actions in Vietnam.

A. The President's Power under Article II of the Constitution Extends to the Actions Currently Undertaken in Vietnam.

Under the Constitution, the President, in addition to being Chief Executive, is Commander in Chief of the Army and Navy. He holds the prime responsibility for the conduct of United States foreign relations. These duties carry very broad powers, including the power to deploy American forces abroad and commit them to military operations when the President deems such action necessary to maintain the security and defense of the United States.

At the Federal Constitutional Convention in 1787, it was originally proposed that Congress have the power "to make war." There were objections that legislative proceedings were too slow for this power to be vested in Congress; it was suggested that the Senate might be a better repository. Madison and Gerry then moved to substitute "to declare war" for "to make war," "leaving to the Executive the power to repel sudden attacks." It was objected that this might make it too easy for the Executive to involve the nation in war, but the motion carried with but one dissenting vote.

In 1787 the world was a far larger place, and the framers probably had in mind attacks upon the United States. In the 20th century, the world has grown much smaller. An attack on a country far from our shores can impinge directly on the nation's security. In the SEATO treaty, for example, it is formally declared that an armed attack against Vietnam would endanger the peace and safety of the United States.

Since the Constitution was adopted there have been at least 125 instances in which the President has ordered the armed forces to take action or maintain positions abroad without obtaining prior congressional authorization, starting with the "undeclared war" with France (1798-1800). For example, President Truman ordered 250,000 troops to Korea during the Korean war of the early 1950's. President Eisenhower dispatched 14,000 troops to Lebanon in 1958.

The Constitution leaves to the President the judgment to determine whether the circumstances of a particular armed attack are so urgent and the potential consequences so threatening to the security of the United States that he should act without formally consulting the Congress.

B. The Southeast Asia Collective Defense Treaty Authorizes the President's Actions.

Under article VI of the United States Constitution, "all Treaties made, or which shall be made, under the Authority of the United States, shall be the supreme Law of the Land." Article IV, paragraph 1, of the SEATO treaty establishes as a matter of law that a Communist armed attack against South Vietnam endangers the peace and safety of the United States. In this same provision the United States has undertaken a commitment in the

SEATO treaty to "act to meet the common danger in accordance with its constitutional processes" in the event of such an attack.

Under our Constitution it is the President who must decide when an armed attack has occurred. He has also the constitutional responsibility for determining what measures of defense are required when the peace and safety of the United States are endangered. If he considers that deployment of U.S. forces to South Vietnam is required, and that military measures against the source of Communist aggression in North Vietnam are necessary, he is constitutionally empowered to take those measures.

The SEATO treaty specifies that each party will act "in accordance with its constitutional processes."

It has recently been argued that the use of land forces in Asia is not authorized under the treaty because their use to deter armed attack was not contemplated at the time the treaty was considered by the Senate. Secretary Dulles testified at that time that we did not intend to establish (1) a land army in Southeast Asia capable of deterring Communist aggression, or (2) an integrated headquarters and military organization like that of NATO; instead, the United States would rely on "mobile striking power" against the sources of aggression. However, the treaty obligation in article IV, paragraph 1, to meet the common danger in the event of armed aggression, is not limited to particular modes of military action. What constitutes an adequate deterrent or an appropriate response, in terms of military strategy, may change; but the essence of our commitment to act to meet the common danger, as necessary at the time of an armed aggression, remains. In 1954 the forecast of military judgment might have been against the use of substantial United States ground forces in Vietnam. But that does not preclude the President from reaching a different military judgment in differing circumstances, 12 years later.

C. The Joint Resolution of Congress of August 10, 1964, Authorizes United States Participation in the Collective Defense of South Vietnam.

As stated earlier, the legality of United States participation in the defense of South Vietnam does not rest on the constitutional power of the President under article II—or indeed on that power taken in conjunction with the SEATO treaty. In addition, the Congress has acted in unmistakable fashion to approve and authorize United States actions in Vietnam.

Following the North Vietnamese attacks in the Gulf of Tonkin against United States destroyers, Congress adopted, by a Senate vote of 88-2 and a House vote of 416-0, a joint resolution containing a series of important declarations and provisions of law.

Section 1 resolved that "the Congress approves and supports the determination of the President, as Commander in Chief, to take all necessary measures to repel any armed attack against the forces of the United

States and to prevent further aggression." Thus, the Congress gave its sanction to specific actions by the President to repel attacks against United States naval vessels in the Gulf of Tonkin and elsewhere in the western Pacific. Congress further approved the taking of "all necessary measures ...to prevent further aggression." This authorization extended to those measures the President might consider necessary to ward off further attacks and to prevent further aggression by North Vietnam in Southeast Asia.

The joint resolution then went on to provide in section 2:

> The United States regards as vital to its national interest and to world peace the maintenance of international peace and security in Southeast Asia. Consonant with the Constitution of the United States and the Charter of the United Nations and in accordance with its obligations under the Southeast Asia Collective Defense Treaty, the United States is, therefore, prepared, as the President determines, to take all necessary steps, including the use of armed force, to assist any member or protocol state of the Southeast Asia Collective Defense Treaty requesting assistance in defense of its freedom.

Section 2 thus constitutes an authorization to the President, in his discretion, to act—using armed force if he determines that it is required—to assist South Vietnam at its request in defense of its freedom. The identification of South Vietnam through the reference to "protocol state" in this section is unmistakable, and the grant of authority "as the President determines" is unequivocal.

It has been suggested that the legislative history of the joint resolution shows an intention to limit United States assistance to South Vietnam to aid, advice, and training. This suggestion is based on an amendment offered from the floor by Senator [Gaylord] Nelson which would have added the following to the text:

> The Congress also approves and supports the efforts of the President to bring the problem of peace in Southeast Asia to the Security Council of the United Nations, and the President's declaration that the United States, seeking no extension of the present military conflict, will respond to provocation in a manner that is "limited and fitting." Our continuing policy is to limit our role to the provision of aid, training assistance, and military advice, and it is the sense of Congress that, except when provoked to a greater response, we should continue to attempt to avoid a direct military involvement in the Southeast Asia conflict.[11]

Senator [J.W.] Fulbright, who had reported the joint resolution from the Foreign Relations Committee, spoke on the amendment as follows:

> It states fairly accurately what the President has said would be our policy, and what I stated my understanding was as to our policy; also what other Senators have stated. In other words, it states that our response should be appropriate and limited to the provocation, which the Senator states as "respond to provocation in a manner that is limited and fitting," and so forth. We do not wish any

political or military bases there. We are not seeking to gain a colony. We seek to insure the capacity of these people to develop along the lines of their own desires, independent of domination by communism.

The Senator has put into his amendment a statement of policy that is unobjectionable. However, I cannot accept the amendment under the circumstances. I do not believe it is contrary to the joint resolution, but it is an enlargement. I am informed that the House is now voting on this resolution. The House joint resolution is about to be presented to us. I cannot accept the amendment and go to conference with it, and thus take responsibility for delaying matters.

I do not object to it as a statement of policy. I believe it is an accurate reflection of what I believe is the President's policy, judging from his own statements. That does not mean that as a practical matter I can accept the amendment. It would delay matters to do so. It would cause confusion and require a conference, and present us with all the other difficulties that are involved in this kind of legislative action. I regret that I cannot do it, even though I do not at all disagree with the amendment as a general statement of policy.[12]

Senator Nelson's amendment related the degree and kind of U.S. response in Vietnam to "provocation" on the other side; the response should be "limited and fitting." The greater the provocation, the stronger are the measures that may be characterized as "limited and fitting." Bombing of North Vietnamese naval bases was a "limited and fitting" response to the attacks on U.S. destroyers in August 1964, and the subsequent actions taken by the United States and South Vietnam have been an appropriate response to the increased war of aggression carried on by North Vietnam since that date. Moreover, Senator Nelson's proposed amendment did not purport to be a restriction on authority available to the President but merely a statement concerning what should be the continuing policy of the United States.

Congressional realization of the scope of authority being conferred by the joint resolution is shown by the legislative history of the measure as a whole. The following exchange between Senators Cooper and Fulbright is illuminating:

Mr. COOPER [John Sherman Cooper]. The Senator will remember that the SEATO Treaty, in article IV, provides that in the event an armed attack is made upon a party to the Southeast Asia Collective Defense Treaty, or upon one of the protocol states such as South Vietnam, the parties to the treaty, one of whom is the United States, would then take such action as might be appropriate, after resorting to their constitutional processes. I assume that would mean, in the case of the United States, that Congress would be asked to grant the authority to act.

Does the Senator consider that in enacting this resolution we are satisfying that requirement of article IV of the Southeast Asia Collective Defense Treaty? In other words, are we now giving the President advance authority to take whatever action he may deem necessary respecting South Vietnam and its defense, or with respect to the defense of any other country included in the treaty?

Mr. FULBRIGHT. I think that is correct.

Mr. COOPER. Then looking ahead, if the President decided that it was necessary to use such force as could lead into war, we will give that authority by this resolution?

Mr. FULBRIGHT. That is the way I would interpret it. If a situation later developed in which we thought the approval should be withdrawn it could be withdrawn by concurrent resolution.[13]

The August 1964 joint resolution continues in force today. Section 2 of the resolution provides that it shall expire "when the President shall determine that the peace and security of the area is reasonably assured by international conditions created by action of the United Nations or otherwise, except that it may be terminated earlier by concurrent resolution of the Congress." The President has made no such determination, nor has Congress terminated the joint resolution.[14]

Instead, Congress in May 1965 approved an appropriation of $700 million to meet the expense of mounting military requirements in Vietnam. (Public Law 89—18, 79 Stat. 109). The President's message asking for this appropriation stated that this was "not a routine appropriation. For each member of Congress who supports this request is also voting to persist in our efforts to halt Communist aggression in South Vietnam." The appropriation act constitutes a clear congressional endorsement and approval of the actions taken by the President.

On March 1, 1966, the Congress continued to express its support of the President's policy by approving a $4.8 billion supplemental military authorization by votes of 392-4 and 93-2. An amendment that would have limited the President's authority to commit forces to Vietnam was rejected in the Senate by a vote of 94-2.

D. No Declaration of War by the Congress Is Required To Authorize United States Participation in the Collective Defense of South Vietnam.

No declaration of war is needed to authorize American actions in Vietnam. As shown in the preceding sections, the President has ample authority to order the participation of United States armed forces in the defense of South Vietnam.

Over a very long period in our history, practice and precedent have confirmed the constitutional authority to engage United States forces in hostilities without a declaration of war. This history extends from the undeclared war with France and the war against the Barbary pirates at the end of the 18th century to the Korean war of 1950-53.

James Madison, one of the leading framers of the Constitution, and Presidents John Adams and Jefferson all construed the Constitution, in their official actions during the early years of the Republic, as authorizing the United States to employ its armed forces abroad in hostilities in the absence of any congressional declaration of war. Their views and actions constitute highly persuasive evidence as to the meaning and effect of the Constitution by the early Presidents and Congresses in regard to the lawfulness of hostilities without a declaration of war. The instances of such action in our history are numerous.

In the Korean conflict, where large-scale hostilities were conducted with an American troop participation of a quarter of a million men, no declaration of war was made by the Congress. The President acted on the basis of his constitutional responsibilities. While the Security Council, under a treaty of this country—the United Nations Charter—recommended assistance to the Republic of Korea against the Communist armed attack, the United States had no treaty commitment at that time obligating us to join in the defense of South Korea. In the case of South Vietnam we have the obligation of the SEATO treaty and clear expressions of congressional support. If the President could act in Korea without a declaration of war, *a fortiori* he is empowered to do so now in Vietnam.

It may be suggested that a declaration of war is the only available constitutional process by which congressional support can be made effective for the use of United States armed forces in combat abroad. But the Constitution does not insist on any rigid formalism. It gives Congress a choice of ways in which to exercise its powers. In the case of Vietnam the Congress has supported the determination of the President by the Senate's approval of the SEATO treaty, the adoption of the joint resolution of August 10, 1964, and the enactment of the necessary authorizations and appropriations.

V. CONCLUSION

South Vietnam is being subjected to armed attack by Communist North Vietnam, through the infiltration of armed personnel, military equipment, and regular combat units. International law recognizes the right of individual and collective self-defense against armed attack. South Vietnam and the United States upon the request of South Vietnam, are engaged in such collective defense of the South. Their actions are in conformity with international law and with the Charter of the United Nations. The fact that South Vietnam has been precluded by Soviet veto from becoming a Member of the United Nations and the fact that South Vietnam is a zone of a temporarily divided state in no way diminish the right of collective defense of South Vietnam.

The United States has commitments to assist South Vietnam in defending itself against Communist aggression from the North. The United States gave undertakings to this effect at the conclusion of the Geneva Conference in 1954. Later that year the United States undertook an international obligation in the SEATO treaty to defend South Vietnam against Communist armed aggression. And during the past decade the

United States has given additional assurances to the South Vietnamese Government.

The Geneva Accords of 1954 provided for a cease fire and regroupment of contending forces, a division of Vietnam into two zones, and a prohibition on the use of either zone for the resumption of hostilities or to "further an aggressive policy." From the beginning, North Vietnam violated the Geneva Accords through a systematic effort to gain control of South Vietnam by force. In the light of these progressive North Vietnamese violations, the introduction into South Vietnam beginning in late 1961 of substantial United States military equipment and personnel, to assist in the defense of the South, was fully justified; substantial breach of an international agreement by one side permits the other side to suspend performance of corresponding obligations under the agreement. South Vietnam was justified in refusing to implement the provisions of the Geneva Accords calling for reunification through free elections throughout the Vietnam since the Communist regime in North Vietnam created conditions in the North that made free elections entirely impossible.

The President of the United States has full authority to commit United States forces in the collective defense of South Vietnam. This authority stems from the constitutional powers of the President. However, it is not necessary to rely on the Constitution alone as the source of the President's authority, since the SEATO treaty—advised and consented to by the Senate and forming part of the law of the land—sets forth a United States commitment to defend South Vietnam against armed attack, and since the Congress—in the joint resolution of August 10, 1964, and in authorization and appropriations acts for support of the U.S. military effort in Vietnam—has given its approval and support to the President's actions. United States actions in Vietnam, taken by the President and approved by the Congress, do not require any declaration of war, as shown by a long line of precedents for the use of United States armed forces abroad in the absence of any congressional declaration of war.

Notes

1. See, *e.g.*, Jessup, *A Modern Law of Nations*, 163 ff. (1948); Oppenheim, *International Law*, 297 ff. (8th ed., Lauterpacht, 1955). And see, generally, Bowett, *Self-Defense in International Law* (1958).

2. While non-Members, such as South Vietnam, have not formally undertaken the obligations of the United Nations Charter as their own treaty obligations, it should be recognized that much of the substantive law of the Charter has become part of the general law of nations through a very wide acceptance by nations the world over. This is particularly true of the Charter provisions bearing on the use of force. Moreover, in the case of South Vietnam, the South Vietnamese Government has expressed its ability and willingness to abide by the Charter, in applying for United Nations Membership. Thus it seems entirely appropriate to appraise the actions of South Vietnam in relation to the legal standards set forth in the United Nations Charter.

3. See 6 UNCIO Documents 459.

4. In particular, the statement of the first purpose, to that end, to take effective collective measures for the prevention and removal of threats to the peace, and for the suppression of acts of aggression or other breaches of the peace, and to bring about by peaceful means, and in conformity with the principles of justice and international law, adjustment or settlement of international disputes or situations which might lead to a breach of the peace ...

5. Bowett, *Self-Defense in International Law*, 193-195 (1958); Goodhart, "The North Atlantic Treaty of 1949," 79 *Recueil Des Cours*, 183, 202-204 (1951, vol. II), quoted in 5 *Whiteman's Digest of International Law*, 1067-1068 (1965); Kelsen, *The Law of the United Nations*; 793 (1950); see Stone, *Aggression and World Order*, 44 (1958).

6. 17 UNCIO Documents 288.

7. An argument has been made by some that the United States, by joining in the collective defense of South Vietnam, has violated the peaceful settlement obligation of article 33 in the Charter. This argument overlooks the obvious proposition that a victim of armed aggression is not required to sustain the attack undefended while efforts are made to find a political solution with the aggressor. Article 51 of the Charter illustrates this by making perfectly clear that the inherent right of self-defense is impaired by "Nothing in the present Charter," including the provisions of article 33.

8. These accords were composed of a bilateral cease-fire agreement between the "Commander-in-Chief of the People's Army of Vietnam" and the "Commander-in-Chief of the French Union Forces in Indochina," to-

gether with a Final Declaration of the Conference, to which France adhered. However, it is to be noted that the South Vietnamese Government was not a signatory of the cease-fire agreement and did not adhere to the Final Declaration. South Vietnam entered a series of reservations in a statement to the conference. This statement was noted by the conference, but by decision of the conference chairman it was not included or referred to in the Final Declaration.

9. This principle of law and the circumstances in which it may be invoked are most fully discussed in the Fourth Report on the Law of Treaties by Sir Gerald Fitzmaurice, articles 18, 20 (U.N. doc. A/CN.4/ 120(1959)) II Yearbook of the International Law Commission 37 (U.N. doc A/CN.4/SER.A/1959/Add.1) and in the later report by Sir Humphrey Waldock, article 20 (U.N. doc. A/CN.4/156 and Add. 1-3 (1963)) II Yearbook of the International Law Commission 36 (U.N. doc. A/CN.4/SER.A/1963/Add.1). Among the authorities cited by the fourth report for this proposition are: II Oppenheim, *International Law* 136, 137 (7th ed. Lauterpacht 1955); I Rousseau, *Principes generaux du droit international public* 365 (1944); II Hyde, *International Law* 1660 et seq. (2d ed. 1947); II Guggenhiem, *Traite de droit international public* 84, 85 (1935); Spiropoulos, *Traite theorique et pratique de droit international public* 289 (1933); Verdross, *Volkerrecht*, 328 (1950); Hall, *Treatise* 21 (8th ed. Higgins 1924); 3 Accioly, *Tratado de Direito Internacional Publico* 82 (1956-57). See also draft article 42 and 46 of the Law of Treaties by the International Law Commission, contained in the report on the work of its 15th session (General Assembly, Official Records, 18th Session, Supplement No. 9 (A/5809)).

10. In any event, if North Vietnam considered there had been a breach of obligation by the South, its remedies lay in discussion with Saigon, perhaps in an appeal to the cochairman of the Geneva Conference, or in a reconvening of the conference to consider the situation. Under international law, North Vietnam had no right to use force outside its own zone in order to secure its political objectives.

11. 110 *Cong. Rec.* 18459 (Aug. 7, 1964).

12. *Ibid.*

13. *Cong. Rec.* 18409 (Aug. 6, 1964). Senator [Wayne] Morse, who opposed the joint resolution, expressed the following view on August 6, 1964, concerning the scope of the proposed resolution:

> "Another Senator thought, in the early part of the debate, that this course would not broaden the power of the President to engage in a land war if he decided that he wanted to apply the resolution in that way.
>
> That Senator was taking great consolation in the then held belief that, if he voted for the resolution, it would give no authority to the President to send many troops into Asia. I am sure he was quite disappointed to finally learn, because it took a little time to get the matter cleared, that the resolution places no

restriction on the President in that respect. If he is still in doubt, let him read the language on page 2, lines 3 to 6, and page 2, lines 11 to 17. The first reads:

The Congress approves and supports the determination of the President, as Commander-in-Chief, to take all necessary measures to repel any armed attack against the forces of the United States and to prevent further aggression.

It does not say he is limited in regard to the sending of ground forces. It does not limit that authority. That is why I have called it a predated declaration of war, in clear violation of article I, section 8, of the Constitution, which vests the power to declare war in the Congress, and not in the President.

What is proposed is to authorize the President of the United States, without a declaration of war, to commit acts of war" (110 *Cong. Rec.* 18426-7 (Aug. 6, 1964)).

14. On March 1, 1966, the Senate voted, 92-5, to table an amendment that would have repealed the joint resolution.

Appendix II

General Treaty for the Renunciation of War (August 27, 1928) (often referred to as "Kellogg-Briand Pact" or "Pact of Paris")

(XXXXVI U.S. Statutes at Large 2343. Ratified by the United States of America on January 17, 1929. Entered into force on July 24, 1929.)

[Preamble]

Article 1

The High Contracting Parties solemnly declare in the names of their respective peoples that they condemn recourse to war for the solution of international controversies, and renounce it as an instrument of national policy in their relations with one another.

Article 2

The High Contracting Parties agree that the settlement or solution of all disputes or conflicts of whatever nature or of whatever origin they may be, which may arise among them, shall never be sought except by pacific means.

Article 3

[Provisions on ratification by the fifteen "High Contracting Parties named in the preamble," which Parties include the United States of America; subsequently, the Treaty is "open ...for adherence by all the other Powers of the world."]

IN FAITH WHEREOF the respective Plenipotentiaries have signed this Treaty ...and hereunto affix their seals.

DONE at Paris, the twenty-seventh day of August in the year one thousand nine hundred and twenty-eight.

[signatories, including
that of Secretary of State
Frank B. Kellogg
for the United States of America]

Appendix III

Charter of the United Nations (June 26, 1945)

(T.S. 993. 59 Stat. 1031. The United States of America deposited its instrument of ratification on August 8, 1945. Entered into force on October 24, 1945.)

We the peoples of the United Nations determined

to save succeeding generations from the scourge of war, which twice in our lifetime has brought untold sorrow to mankind, and

to reaffirm faith in fundamental human rights, in the dignity and worth of the human person, in the equal rights of men and women and of nations large and small, and

to establish conditions under which justice and respect for the obligations arising from treaties and other sources of international law can be maintained, and

to promote social progress and better standards of life in larger freedom,

and for these ends

to practice tolerance and live together in peace with one another as good neighbors, and

to unite our strength to maintain international peace and security, and

to ensure, by the acceptance of principles and the institution of methods, that armed force shall not be used, save in the common interest,

have resolved to combine our efforts to accomplish these aims.

CHAPTER I
PURPOSES AND PRINCIPLES

Article 1

The Purposes of the United Nations are:

1. To maintain international peace and security, and to that end: to take effective collective measures for the prevention and removal of threats to the peace, and for the suppression of acts of aggression or other breaches of the peace, and to bring about by peaceful means, and in conformity with the principles of justice and international law, adjustment or settlement of international disputes or situations which might lead to a breach of the peace;

2. To develop friendly relations among nations based on respect for the principles of equal rights and self-determination of peoples, and to take other appropriate measures to strengthen universal peace;

Article 2

The Organization and its Members, in pursuit of the Purposes stated in Article 1, shall act in accordance with the following Principles.

...

2. All Members, in order to ensure to all of them the rights and benefits resulting from Membership, shall fulfill in good faith the obligations assumed by them in accordance with the present Charter.

3. All Members shall settle their international disputes by peaceful means in such a manner that international peace and security, and justice, are not endangered.

4. All Members shall refrain in their international relations from the threat or use of force against the territorial integrity or political independence of any state, or in any other manner inconsistent with the Purposes of the United Nations.

...

7. Nothing contained in the present Charter shall authorize the United Nations to intervene in matters which are essentially within the domestic jurisdiction of any state or shall require the Members to submit such matters to settlement under the present Charter; but this principle shall not prejudice the application of enforcement measures under Chapter VII.

CHAPTER V
THE SECURITY COUNCIL

...

Functions and Powers

Article 24

1. In order to ensure prompt and effective action by the United Nations, its Members confer on the Security Council primary responsibility for the maintenance of international peace and security, and agree that in carrying out its duties under this responsibility the Security Council acts on their behalf.

2. In discharging these duties the Security Council shall act in accordance with the Purposes and Principles of the United Nations.

...

Procedure

...

Article 32

Any Member of the United Nations which is not a Member of the Security Council or any state which is not a Member of the United Nations, if it is a party to a dispute under consideration by the Security Council, shall be invited to participate, without vote, in the discussion relating to the dispute.

CHAPTER VI
PACIFIC SETTLEMENT OF DISPUTE

Article 33

1. The parties to any dispute, the continuance of which is likely to endanger the maintenance of international peace and security, shall, first of all, seek a solution by negotiation, enquiry, mediation, conciliation, arbitration, judicial settlement, resort to regional agencies or arrangements, or other peaceful means of their own choice.

...

Article 35

...

2. A state which is not a Member of the United Nations may bring to the attention of the Security Council or of the General Assembly any

dispute to which it is a party if it accepts in advance, for the purposes of the dispute, the obligations of pacific settlement provided in the present Charter.

...

Article 37

1. Should the parties to a dispute of the nature referred to in Article 33 fail to settle it by the means indicated in that Article, they shall refer it to the Security Council.

...

CHAPTER VII
ACTION WITH RESPECT TO THREATS TO THE PEACE, BREACHES OF THE PEACE, AND ACTS OF AGGRESSION

Article 39

The Security Council shall determine the existence of any threat to the peace, breach of the peace, or act of aggression and shall make recommendations, or decide what measures shall be taken in accordance with Articles 41 and 42, to maintain or restore international peace and security.

...

Article 41

The Security Council may decide what measures not involving the use of armed force are to be employed to give effect to its decisions, and it may call upon the Members of the United Nations to apply such measures. These may include complete or partial interruption of economic relations and of rail, sea, air, postal, telegraphic, radio, and other means of communication, and the severance of diplomatic relations.

Article 42

Should the Security Council consider that measures provided for in Article 41 would be inadequate or have proved to be inadequate, it may take such action by air, sea, or land forces as may be necessary to maintain or restore international peace and security. Such action may include demonstrations, blockade, and other operations by air, sea, or land forces of Members of the United Nations.

Article 43

[Refers to future agreements by which Members would undertake *obligations* to make armed forces and other military assistance available to the Security Council.]

Article 44

When the Security Council has decided to use force it shall, before calling upon a Member not represented on it to provide armed forces in fulfillment of the obligations assumed under Article 43, invite that Member, if the Member so desires, to participate in the decisions of the Security Council concerning the employment of contingents of the Member's armed forces.

...

Article 51

Nothing in the present Charter shall impair the inherent right of individual or collective self-defense if an armed attack occurs against a Member of the United Nations, until the Security Council has taken the measures necessary to maintain international peace and security. Measures taken by Members in the exercise of this right of self-defense shall be immediately reported to the Security Council and shall not in any way affect the authority and responsibility of the Security Council under the present Charter to take at any time such action as it deems necessary in order to maintain or restore international peace and security.

CHAPTER VIII
REGIONAL ARRANGEMENTS

Article 52

1. Nothing in the present Charter precludes the existence of regional arrangements or agencies dealing with such matters relating to the maintenance of international peace and security as are appropriate for regional action, provided that such arrangements or agencies and their activities are consistent with the Purposes and Principles of the United Nations.

2. The Members of the United Nations entering into such arrangements or constituting such agencies shall make every effort to achieve pacific settlement of local disputes through such regional arrangements or by such regional agencies before referring them to the Security Council.

3. The Security Council shall encourage the development of pacific settlement of local disputes through such regional arrangements or by such regional agencies either on the initiative of the states concerned or by reference from the Security Council.

...

Article 53

1. The Security Council shall, where appropriate, utilize such regional arrangements or agencies for enforcement action under its authority.

But no enforcement action shall be taken under regional arrangements or by regional agencies without the authorization of the Security Council. [The rest of this Article refers to States which during the Second World War were enemies of any signatory of the Charter, and is therefore not pertinent to the Vietnam situation.]

Article 54

The Security Council shall at all times be kept fully informed of activities undertaken or in contemplation under regional arrangements or by regional agencies for the maintenance of international peace and security.

...

CHAPTER XVI
MISCELLANEOUS PROVISIONS

Article 103

In the event of a conflict between the obligations of the Members of the United Nations under the present Charter and their obligations under any other international agreement, their obligations under the present Charter shall prevail.

...

CHAPTER XIX
RATIFICATION AND SIGNATURE

Article 110

1. The present Charter shall be ratified by the signatory states in accordance with their respective constitutional processes.

2. The ratification shall be deposited with the Government of the United States of America ...

3. The present Charter shall come into force upon the deposit of ratifications by the Republic of China, France, the Union of Soviet Socialist Republics, the United Kingdom of Great Britain and Northern Ireland, and the United States of America, and by a majority of the other signatory states.

4. The states signatory to the present Charter which ratify it after it has come into force will become original Members of the United Nations on the date of the deposit of their respective ratifications.

Article 111

The present Charter shall remain deposited in the archives of the Government of the United States of America.

IN FAITH WHEREOF the representatives of the Governments of the United Nations have signed the present Charter.

DONE at the city of San Francisco the twenty-sixth day of June, one thousand nine hundred and forty-five.

[signatories, including the following
for the United States of America:
Edward R. Stettinius, Cordell Hull,
Tom Connally, A.H. Vandenberg,
Saul Bloom, Charles A. Eaton,
Harold E. Stassen, Virginia C. Gildersleeve]

Appendix IV

Geneva Accords of 1954

At the closing session of the Geneva Conference (July 21, 1954), the participants had nine documents in front of them: three agreements, signed the night before, on the cessation of hostilities "in Vietnam," "in Laos" and "in Cambodia," respectively; five unilateral declarations, issued by the Governments of Laos, of Cambodia and of the French Republic, respectively; and a draft "Final Declaration" which in the words of the Chairman of the session, Mr. Anthony Eden (United Kingdom), "takes note of all these eight documents." Mr. Eden then asked his "colleagues in turn to express themselves upon this Declaration."

The representatives of France, the People's Republic of China, the United Kingdom, and the Soviet Union stated as follows:

M. Mendes-France: "Mr. Chairman, the French Delegation approves the terms of this Declaration."

Mr. Chou En-lai: "We agree."

Mr. Eden: "On behalf of Her Majesty's Government in the United Kingdom, I associate myself with the final Declaration of this Conference."

Mr. Molotov: "The Soviet Delegation agrees."

The statement made by Mr. Bedell-Smith on behalf of the United States of America is quoted below, after the text of the bilateral Agreement on Vietnam and the text of the Final Declaration.

It may be useful to point out that the French-Viet Minh Agreement on the cessation of hostilities in Vietnam established *inter alia* two different organs for the execution of the Agreement (see Articles 28-47): (a) a "Joint Commission," composed of officers of the two sides—the French forces and the Viet Minh forces—that had just concluded the armistice agreement, and (b) a Commission composed of representatives of outside States—India, Canada and Poland—called "International Commission for Supervision and Control in Vietnam," that has become known as "International Control Commission" or I.C.C.

(The above quotations and the texts that follow are reproduced from "*Further Documents Relating to the Discussion of Indochina at the Geneva Conference.*" Cmd. 9239, Miscellaneous No. 20 (1954). Her Majesty's Stationery Office, London, 5-11, 27-38.)

AGREEMENT ON THE CESSATION OF HOSTILITIES IN VIETNAM

[concluded between the Commanders-in-Chief of the French Union Forces in Indochina and of the People's Army of Vietnam on July 20, 1954]

CHAPTER 1
PROVISIONAL MILITARY DEMARCATION LINE AND DEMILITARIZED ZONE

Article 1

A provisional military demarcation line shall be fixed, on either side of which the forces of the two parties shall be regrouped after their withdrawal, the forces of the People's Army of Vietnam to the north of the line and the forces of the French Union to the south.

The provisional military demarcation line is fixed as shown on the map attached (see Map No. 1). [not reproduced]

It is also agreed that a demilitarized zone shall be established on either side of the demarcation line, to a width of not more than 5 kms. from it, to act as a buffer zone and avoid any incidents which might result in the resumption of hostilities.

Article 2

The period within which the movement of all forces of either party into its regrouping zone on either side of the provisional military demarcation line shall be completed shall not exceed three hundred (300) days from the date of the present Agreement's entry into force.

Article 3

When the provisional military demarcation line coincides with a waterway, the waters of such waterway shall be open to civil navigation by both parties wherever one bank is controlled by one party and the other bank by the other party. The Joint Commission shall establish rules of navigation for the stretch of waterway in question. The merchant shipping and other civilian craft of each party shall have unrestricted access to the land under its military control.

Article 4

The provisional military demarcation line between the two final regrouping zones is extended into the territorial waters by a line perpendicular to the general line of the coast. All coastal islands north of this boundary shall be evacuated by the armed forces of the French Union, and all islands south of it shall be evacuated by the forces of the People's Army of Vietnam.

Article 5

To avoid any incidents which might result in the resumption of hostilities, all military forces, supplies, and equipment shall be withdrawn from the demilitarized zone within twenty-five (25) days of the present Agreement's entry into force.

Article 6

No person, military or civilian, shall be permitted to cross the provisional military demarcation line unless specifically authorized to do so by the Joint Commission.

Article 7

No person, military or civilian, shall be permitted to enter the demilitarized zone except persons concerned with the conduct of civil administration and relief and persons specifically authorized to enter by the Joint Commission.

Article 8

Civil administration and relief in the demilitarized zone on either side of the provisional military demarcation line shall be the responsibility of the Commander-in-Chief of the two parties in their respective zones. The numbers of persons, military or civilian, from each side who are permitted to enter the demilitarized zone for the conduct of civil administration and relief shall be determined by the respective Commanders, but in no case shall the total number authorized by either side exceed at any one time a figure to be determined by the Trung Gia Military Commission or by the Joint Commission. The number of civil police and the arms to be carried by them shall be determined by the Joint Commission. No one else shall carry arms unless specifically authorized to do so by the Joint Commission.

Article 9

Nothing contained in this chapter shall be construed as limiting the complete freedom of movement—into, out of, or within the demilitarized zone—of the Joint Commission, its joint groups, the International Commission to be set up as indicated below, its inspection teams and any other persons, supplies, or equipment specifically authorized to enter the demilitarized zone by the Joint Commission. Freedom of movement shall be permitted across the territory under the military control of either side over any road or waterway which has to be taken between points within the demilitarized zone when such points are not connected by roads or waterways lying completely within the demilitarized zone.

CHAPTER II
PRINCIPLES AND PROCEDURE GOVERNING IMPLEMENTATION OF THE PRESENT AGREEMENT

Article 10

The Commanders of the Forces on each side, on the one side the Commander-in-Chief of the French Union forces in Indochina and on the other side the Commander-in-Chief of the People's Army of Vietnam, shall order and enforce the complete cessation of all hostilities in Vietnam by all armed forces under their control, including all units and personnel of the ground, naval, and air forces.

Article 11

In accordance with the principle of a simultaneous cease-fire throughout Indochina, the cessation of hostilities shall be simultaneous throughout all parts of Vietnam, in all areas of hostilities and for all the forces of the two parties.

Taking into account the time effectively required to transmit the cease-fire order down to the lowest echelons of the combatant forces on both sides, the two parties are agreed that the cease-fire shall take effect completely and simultaneously for the different sections of the country as follows:

Northern Vietnam at 8.00 a.m. (local time) on July 27, 1954
Central Vietnam at 8.00 a.m. (local time) on August 1, 1954
Southern Vietnam at 8.00 a.m. (local time) on August 11, 1954

From such time as the cease-fire becomes effective in North Vietnam, both parties undertake not to engage in any large-scale offensive action in any part of the Indochinese theatre of operations and not to commit the air forces based on North Vietnam outside that sector. The two parties also undertake to inform each other of their plans for movement from one regrouping zone to another within twenty-five (25) days of the present Agreement's entry into force.

Article 12

All the operations and movements entailed in the cessation of hostilities and regrouping must proceed in a safe and orderly fashion: [follow provisions on removal of mines, and on the regrouping of the forces of the two parties.]

Article 13

[Provisions on temporary military air-corridors]

Article 14

Political and administrative measures in the two regrouping zones, on either side of the provisional military demarcation line:

(a) Pending the general elections which will bring about the unification of Vietnam, the conduct of civil administration in each regrouping zone shall be in the hands of the party whose forces are to be regrouped there in virtue of the present Agreement.

(b) Any territory controlled by one party which is transferred to the other party by the regrouping plan shall continue to be administered by the former party until such date as all the troops who are to be transferred have completely left that territory so as to free the zone assigned to the party in question. From then on, such territory shall be regarded as transferred to the other party, who shall assume responsibility for it.

Steps shall be taken to ensure that there is no break in the transfer of responsibilities. For this purpose, adequate notice shall be given by the withdrawing party to the other party, which shall make the necessary arrangements, in particular by sending administrative and police detachments to prepare for the assumption of administrative responsibility. The length of such notice shall be determined by the Trung Gia Military Commission. The transfer shall be effected in successive stages for the various territorial sectors.

The transfer of the civil administration of Hanoi and Haiphong to the authorities of the Democratic Republic of Vietnam shall be completed within the respective time-limits laid down in Article 15 for military movements.

(c) Each party undertakes to refrain from any reprisals or discrimination against persons or organizations on account of their activities during the hostilities and to guarantee their democratic liberties.

(d) From the date of entry into force of the present Agreement until the movement of troops is completed, any civilians residing in a district controlled by one party who wish to go and live in the zone assigned to the other party shall be permitted and helped to do so by the authorities in that district.

Article 15

The disengagement of the combatants, and the withdrawals and transfers of military forces, equipment, and supplies shall take place in accordance with the following principles:

(a) The withdrawals and transfers of the military forces, equipment and supplies of the two parties shall be completed within three hundred (300) days, as laid down in Article 2 of the present Agreement;

(b) Within either territory successive withdrawals shall be made by sectors, portions of sectors, or provinces. Transfers from one regrouping zone to another shall be made in successive monthly installments proportionate to the number of troops to be transferred;

(c) The two parties shall undertake to carry out all troop withdrawals and transfers in accordance with the aims of the present Agreement, shall permit no hostile act, and shall take no step whatsoever which might hamper such withdrawals and transfers. They shall assist one another as far as this is possible;

(d) the two parties shall permit no destruction or sabotage of any public property and no injury to the life and property of the civil population. They shall permit no interference in local civil administrations;

(e) The Joint Commission and the International Commission shall ensure that steps are taken to safeguard the forces in the course of withdrawal and transfer;

(f) The Trung Gia Military Commission, and later the Joint Commission, shall determine by common agreement the exact procedure for the disengagement of the combatants and for troop withdrawals and transfers, on the basis of the principles mentioned above and within the framework laid down below:

> 1. The disengagement of the combatants ...shall be completed within a period not exceeding fifteen (15) days after the date when the cease-fire becomes effective. [follow details]
>
> 2. The withdrawals and transfers shall be effected in the following order and within the following periods from the date of the entry into force of the present Agreement:

Forces of the French Union

Hanoi perimeter 80days
Haiduong perimeter .... 100 days
Haiphong perimeter .... 300 days

Forces of the People's Army of Vietnam

Ham Tan Xuyenmoc provisional assembly area .... 80 days
Central Vietnam provisional assembly area—
first instalment .... 80 days
Plaine des Joncs provisional assembly area .... 100 days
Central Vietnam provisional assembly area—
second instalment .... 100 days
Pointe Camau provisional assembly area .... 200 days
Central Vietnam provisional assembly area—
last installment .... 300 days

CHAPTER III
BAN ON THE INTRODUCTION OF FRESH TROOPS, MILITARY PERSONNEL, ARMS, AND MUNITIONS, MILITARY BASES

Article 16

With effect from the date of entry into force of the present Agreement, the introduction into Vietnam of any troop reinforcements and additional military personnel is prohibited.

It is understood, however, that the rotation of units and groups of personnel, the arrival in Vietnam of individual personnel on a temporary duty basis, and the return to Vietnam of the individual personnel after short periods of leave or temporary duty outside Vietnam shall be permitted under the conditions laid down below:

(a) Rotation of units (defined in paragraph (c) of this Article) and groups of personnel shall not be permitted for French Union troops stationed north of the provisional military demarcation line laid down in Article 1 of the present Agreement during the withdrawal period provided for in Article 2.

However, under the heading of individual personnel not more than fifty (50) men, including officers, shall during any one month be permitted to enter that part of the country north of the provisional military demarcation line on a temporary duty basis or to return there after short periods of leave or temporary duty outside Vietnam.

(b) "Rotation" is defined as the replacement of units or groups of personnel by other units of the same echelon or by personnel who are arriving in Vietnam territory to do their overseas service there.

(c) The units rotated shall never be larger than a battalion—or the corresponding echelon for air and naval forces.

(d) Rotation shall be conducted on a man-for-man basis, provided, however, that in any one quarter neither party shall introduce more than fifteen thousand five hundred (15,500) members of its armed forces into Vietnam under the rotation policy.

(e) Rotation units (defined in paragraph (c) of this Article) and groups of personnel, and the individual personnel mentioned in this Article, shall enter and leave Vietnam only through the entry points enumerated in Article 20 below.

(f) Each party shall notify the Joint Commission and the International Commission at least two days in advance of any arrivals or departures of units, groups of personnel, and individual personnel in or from Vietnam. Reports on the arrivals or departures of units, groups of personnel, and individual personnel in or from Vietnam shall be submitted daily to the Joint Commission and the International Commission.

All the above-mentioned notifications and reports shall indicate the places and dates of arrival or departure and the number of persons arriving or departing.

(g) The International Commission, through its Inspection Teams, shall supervise and inspect the rotation of units and groups of personnel and the arrival and departure of individual personnel as authorized above at the points of entry enumerated in Article 20 below.

Article 17

(a) With effect from the date of entry into force of the present Agreement, the introduction into Vietnam of any reinforcements in the form of all types of arms, munitions and other war material, such as combat aircraft, naval craft, pieces of ordnance, jet engines and jet weapons, and armored vehicles, is prohibited.

(b) It is understood, however, that war material, arms, and munitions which have been destroyed, damaged, worn out, or used up after the cessation of hostilities may be replaced on the basis of piece-for-piece of the same type and with similar characteristics. Such replacements of war material, arms, and ammunitions shall not be permitted for French Union troops stationed north of the provisional military demarcation line laid down in Article 1 of the present Agreement, during the withdrawal period provided for in Article 2.

Naval craft may perform transport operations between the regrouping zones.

(c) The war material, arms, and munitions for replacement purposes provided for in paragraph (b) of this Article, shall be introduced into Vietnam only through the points of entry enumerated in Article 20 below. War material, arms, and munitions to be replaced shall be shipped from Vietnam only through the points of entry enumerated in Article 20 below.

(d) Apart from the replacements permitted within the limits laid down in paragraph (b) of this Article, the introduction of war material, arms, and munitions of all types in the form of unassembled parts for subsequent assembly is prohibited.

(e) Each party shall notify the Joint Commission and the International Commission at least two days in advance of any arrivals or departures which may take place of war material, arms, and munitions of all types.

In order to justify the requests for the introduction into Vietnam of arms, munitions, and other war material (as defined in paragraph (a) of this Article) for replacement purposes, a report concerning each incoming shipment shall be submitted to the Joint Commission and the International Commission. Such reports shall indicate the use made of the items so replaced.

(f) The International Commission, through its Inspection Teams, shall supervise and inspect the replacements permitted in the circumstances laid down in this Article.

Article 18

With effect from the date of entry into force of the present Agreement, the establishment of new military bases is prohibited throughout Vietnam territory.

Article 19

With effect from the date of entry into force of the present Agreement, no military base under the control of a foreign State may be established in the regrouping zone of either party; the two parties shall ensure that the zones assigned to them do not adhere to any military alliance and are not used for the resumption of hostilities or to further an aggressive policy.

Article 20

The points of entry into Vietnam for rotation personnel and replacements of material are fixed as follows:

—Zones to the north of the provisional military demarcation line: Laokay, Langson, Tien-Yen, Haiphong, Vinh, Dong Hoi, Muong-Sen;

—Zones to the south of the provisional military demarcation line: Tourane, Quinhon, Nhatrang, Bangoi, Saigon, Cap St. Jacques, Tanchau.

CHAPTER IV
PRISONERS OF WAR AND CIVILIAN INTERNEES

Article 21

The liberation and repatriation of all prisoners of war and civilian internees detained by each of the two parties at the coming into force of the present Agreement shall be carried out under the following conditions:

(a) All prisoners of war and civilian internees of Vietnam, French, and other nationalities captured since the beginning of hostilities in Vietnam during military operations or in any other circumstances of war and in any part of the territory of Vietnam shall be liberated within a period of thirty (30) days after the date when the cease-fire becomes effective in each theater.

(b) The term "civilian internees" is understood to mean all persons who, having in any way contributed to the political and armed struggle between the two parties, have been arrested for that reason and have been kept in detention by either party during the period of hostilities.

(c) All prisoners of war and civilian internees held by either party shall be surrendered to the appropriate authorities of the other party, who shall give them all possible assistance in proceeding to their country of origin, place of habitual residence, or the zone of their choice.

CHAPTER V
MISCELLANEOUS

Article 22

The Commanders of the Forces of the two parties shall ensure that persons under their respective commands who violate any of the provisions of the present Agreement are suitably punished.

Article 23

[Provisions on removal of bodies of deceased military personnel of either party (French Union forces and Viet Minh forces).]

Article 24

The present Agreement shall apply to all the armed forces of either party. The armed forces of each party shall respect the demilitarized zone and the territory under the military control of the other party, and shall commit no act and undertake no operation against the other party and shall not engage in blockade of any kind in Vietnam.

For the purposes of the present Article, the word "territory" includes territorial waters and air space.

Article 25

The Commanders of the Forces of the two parties shall afford full protection and all possible assistance and co-operation to the Joint Commission and its joint groups and to the International Commission and its Inspection Teams in the performance of the functions and tasks assigned to them by the present Agreement.

Article 26

The costs involved in the operations of the Joint Commission and joint groups and of the International Commission and its Inspection Teams shall be shared equally between the two parties.

Article 27

The signatories of the present Agreement and their successors in their functions shall be responsible for ensuring the observance and enforcement of the terms and provisions thereof. The Commanders of the Forces of the two parties shall, within their respective commands, take all steps and make all arrangements necessary to ensure full compliance with all the provisions of the present Agreement by all elements and military personnel under their command.

CHAPTER VI
JOINT COMMISSION AND INTERNATIONAL COMMISSION FOR SUPERVISION AND CONTROL IN VIETNAM

Article 28

Responsibility for the execution of the agreement on the cessation of hostilities shall rest with the parties.

Article 29

An International Commission shall ensure the control and supervision of this execution.

Article 30

In order to facilitate, under the conditions shown below, the execution of provisions concerning joint actions by the two parties, a Joint Commission shall be set up in Vietnam.

Article 31

The Joint Commission shall be composed of an equal number of representatives of the Commanders of the two parties.

Article 32

The Presidents of the delegations to the Joint Commission shall hold the rank of General.

The Joint Commission shall set up joint groups the number of which shall be determined by mutual agreement between the two parties. The joint groups shall be composed of an equal number of officers from both parties. Their location on the demarcation line between the regrouping zones shall be determined by the parties whilst taking into account the powers of the Joint Commission.

Article 33

The Joint Commission shall ensure the execution of the following provisions of the Agreement on the cessation of hostilities:

(a) A simultaneous and general cease-fire in Vietnam for all regular and irregular armed forces of the two parties.

(b) A regroupment of the armed forces of the two parties.

(c) Observance of the demarcation lines between the regrouping zones and of the demilitarized sectors.

Within the limits of its competence it shall help the parties to execute the said provisions, shall ensure liaison between them for the purpose of preparing and carrying out plans for the application of these provisions, and shall endeavor to solve such disputed questions as may arise between the parties in the course of executing these provisions.

Article 34

An International Commission shall be set up for the control and supervision over the application of the provisions of the agreement on the cessation of hostilities in Vietnam. It shall be composed of representatives of the following States: Canada, India, and Poland.

It shall be presided over by the Representative of India.

Article 35

The International Commission shall set up Fixed and Mobile Inspection Teams, composed of an equal number of officers appointed by each of the above-mentioned States. The Fixed Teams shall be located at the following points: Laokay, Langson, Tien-Yen, Haiphong, Vinh, Dong Hoi, Muong-Sen, Tourane, Quinhon,Nhatrang, Bangoi, Saigon, Cap St. Jacques, Tanchau. These points of location may, at a later date, be altered at the request of the Joint Commission, or of one of the parties, or of the International Commission itself, by agreement between the International Commission and the command of the party concerned. The zones of action of the Mobile Teams shall be the regions bordering the land and sea frontiers of Vietnam, the demarcation lines between the regrouping zones and the demilitarized zones. Within the limits of these zones they shall have the right to move freely and shall receive from the local civil and military authorities all facilities they may require for the fulfillment of their tasks (provision of personnel, placing at their disposal documents needed for supervision, summoning witnesses necessary for holding inquiries, ensuring the security and freedom of movement of the Inspection Teams, etc.) ...They shall have at their disposal such modern means of transport, observation, and communication as they may require. Beyond the zones of action as defined above, the Mobile Team may, by agreement with the command of the party concerned, carry out other movements within the limits of the tasks given them by the present agreement.

Article 36

The International Commission shall be responsible for supervising the proper execution by the parties of the provisions of the agreement. For this purpose it shall fulfill the tasks of control, observation, inspection, and investigation connected with the application of the provisions of the agreement on the cessation of hostilities, and it shall in particular:

(a) Control the movement of the armed forces of the two parties, effected within the framework of the regroupment plan.

(b) Supervise the demarcation lines between the regrouping areas, and also demilitarized zones.

(c) Control the operations of releasing prisoners of war and civilian internees.

(d) Supervise at ports and airfields as well as along all frontiers of Vietnam the execution of the provisions of the agreement on the cessation of hostilities, règulating the introduction into the country of armed forces, military personnel and of all kinds of arms, munitions, and war material.

Article 37

The International Commission shall, through the medium of the Inspection Teams mentioned above, and as soon as possible either on its own initiative, or at the request of the Joint Commission, or of one of the parties, undertake the necessary investigations both documentary and on the ground.

Article 38

The Inspection Teams shall submit to the International Commission the results of their supervision, their investigation, and their observations; furthermore, they shall draw up such special reports as they may consider necessary or as may be requested from them by the Commission. In the case of a disagreement within the teams, the conclusions of each member shall be submitted to the Commission.

Article 39

If any one Inspection Team is unable to settle an incident or considers that there is a violation or a threat of a serious violation the International Commission shall be informed; the latter shall study the reports and the conclusions of the Inspection Teams and shall inform the parties of the measures which should be taken for the settlement of the incident, ending of the violation, or removal of the threat of violation.

Article 40

When the Joint Commission is unable to reach an agreement on the interpretation to be given to some provision or on the appraisal of a fact, the International Commission shall be informed of the disputed question. Its recommendations shall be sent directly to the parties and shall be notified to the Joint Commission.

Article 41

The recommendations of the International Commission shall be adopted by majority vote, subject to the provisions contained in Article 42. If the votes are divided the chairman's vote shall be decisive.

Article 42

The International Commission may formulate recommendations concerning amendments and additions which should be made to the provisions of the Agreement on the cessation of hostilities in Vietnam, in order to ensure a more effective execution of that Agreement. These recommendations shall be adopted unanimously.

Article 43

When dealing with questions concerning violations, or threats of violations which might lead to a resumption of hostilities, namely:

(a) Refusal by the armed forces of one party to effect the movements provided for in the regroupment plan;

(b) Violation by the armed forces of one of the parties of the regrouping zones, territorial waters, or air space of the other party;

the decisions of the International Commission must be unanimous.

Article 44

If one of the parties refuses to put into effect a recommendation of the International Commission, the parties concerned or the Commission itself shall inform the members of the Geneva Conference.

If the International Commission does not reach unanimity in the cases provided for in Article 42, it shall submit a majority report and one or more minority reports to the members of the Conference.

The International Commission shall inform the members of the Conference in all cases where its activity is being hindered.

Article 45

The International Commission shall be set up at the time of the cessation of hostilities in Indochina in order that it should be able to fulfill the tasks provided for in Article 36.

Article 46

The International Commission for Supervision and Control in Vietnam shall act in close co-operation with the International Commission for Supervision and Control in Cambodia and Laos.

The Secretaries-General of these three Commissions shall be responsible for coordinating their work and for relations between them.

Article 47

The International Commission for Supervision and Control in Vietnam may after consultation with the International Commissions for Supervision and Control in Cambodia and Laos, and having regard to the development of the situation in Cambodia and Laos, progressively reduce its activities. Such a decision must be adopted unanimously.

DONE in Geneva at 2400 hours on the 20th of July, 1954, in French and in Vietnamese, both texts being equally authentic.

For the Commander-in-Chief of the French Union Forces in Indochina:

[Henri] DELTIEL,
Brigadier-General

For the Commander-in-Chief of the People's Army of Vietnam:

TA QUANG BUU,
Vice Minister of National Defense
of the Democratic Republic of Vietnam.

FINAL DECLARATION OF GENEVA CONFERENCE, July 21, 1954

Final declaration, dated July 21, 1954, of the Geneva Conference on the problem of restoring peace in Indochina, in which the representatives of Cambodia, the Democratic Republic of Vietnam, France, Laos, the People's Republic of China, the State of Vietnam, the Union of Soviet Socialist Republics, the United Kingdom, and the United states of America took part.

1. The Conference takes note of the agreements ending hostilities in Cambodia, Laos, and Vietnam and organizing international control and the supervision of the execution of the provisions of these agreements.

2. The Conference expresses satisfaction at the ending of hostilities in Cambodia, Laos, and Vietnam; the Conference expresses its conviction that the execution of the provisions set out in the present declaration and in the agreements on the cessation of hostilities will permit Cambodia, Laos, and Vietnam henceforth to play their part, in full independence and sovereignty, in the peaceful community of nations.

3. The Conference takes note of the declarations made by the governments of Cambodia and of Laos of their intention to adopt measures permitting all citizens to take their place in the national community, in particular by participating in the next general elections, which, in conformity with the constitution of each of these countries, shall take place in the course of the year 1955, by secret ballot and in conditions of respect for fundamental freedoms.

4. The Conference takes note of the clauses in the agreement on the cessation of hostilities in Vietnam prohibiting the introduction into Vietnam of foreign troops and military personnel as well as of all kinds of arms and munitions. The Conference also takes note of the declarations made by the governments of Cambodia and Laos of their resolution not to request foreign aid, whether in war material, in personnel or in instructors except for the purpose of the effective defence of their territory and, in the case of Laos, to the extent defined by the agreements on the cessation of hostilities in Laos.

5. The Conference takes note of the clauses in the agreement on the cessation of hostilities in Vietnam to the effect that no military base under the control of a foreign state may be established in the regrouping zones of the two parties, the latter having the obligation to see that the zones allotted to them shall not constitute part of any military alliance and shall not be utilized for the resumption of hostilities or in the service of an aggressive policy. The Conference also takes note of the declarations of the governments of Cambodia and Laos to the effect that they will not join in any agreement with other states if this agreement includes the obligation to participate in a military alliance not in conformity with the principles

of the Charter of the United Nations or, in the case of Laos, with the principles of the agreement on the cessation of hostilities in Laos or, so long as their security is not threatened, the obligation to establish bases on Cambodian or Laotian territory for the military forces of foreign Powers.

6. The Conference recognizes that the essential purpose of the agreement relating to Vietnam is to settle military questions with a view to ending hostilities and that the military demarcation line is provisional and should not in any way be interpreted as constituting a political or territorial boundary. The Conference expresses its conviction that the execution of the provisions set out in the present declaration and in the agreement on cessation of hostilities creates the necessary basis for the achievement in the near future of a political settlement in Vietnam.

7. The Conference declares that, so far as Vietnam is concerned, the settlement of political problems, effected on the basis of respect for the principles of independence, unity and territorial integrity, shall permit Vietnamese people to enjoy the fundamental freedoms, guaranteed by democratic institutions established as a result of free general elections by secret ballot. In order to ensure that sufficient progress in the restoration of peace has been made, and that all the necessary conditions obtain for free expression of the national will, general elections shall be held in July, 1956, under the supervision of an international commission composed of representatives of the Member States of the International Supervisory Commission, referred to in the agreement on the cessation of hostilities. Consultations will be held on this subject between the competent representative authorities of the two zones from 20 July 1955 onwards.

8. The provisions of the agreements on the cessation of hostilities intended to ensure the protection of individuals and of property must be most strictly applied and must, in particular, allow everyone in Vietnam to decided freely in which zone he wishes to live.

9. The competent representative authorities of the Northern and Southern zones of Vietnam, as well as the authorities of Laos and Cambodia, must not permit any individual or collective reprisals against persons who have collaborated in any way with one of the parties during the war, or against members of such persons' families.

10. The Conference takes note of the declaration of the government of the French Republic to the effect that it is ready to withdraw its troops from the territory of Cambodia, Laos, and Vietnam, at the request of the governments concerned and within periods which shall be fixed by agreement between the parties except in the cases where, by agreement between the two parties, a certain number of French troops shall remain at specified points and for a specified time.

11. The Conference takes note of the declaration of the French government to the effect that for the settlement of all the problems connected with the re-establishment and consolidation of peace in Cambodia, Laos, and Vietnam, the French government will proceed from the principles of

respect for the independence and sovereignty, unity and territorial integrity of Cambodia, Laos, and Vietnam.

12. In their relations with Cambodia, Laos, and Vietnam, each member of the Geneva Conference undertakes to respect the sovereignty, the independence, the unity, and the territorial integrity of the above-mentioned states, and to refrain from any interference in their internal affairs.

13. The members of the Conference agree to consult one another on any question which may be referred to them by the International Supervisory Commission in order to study such measures as may prove necessary to ensure that the agreements on the cessation of hostilities in Cambodia, Laos, and Vietnam are respected.

STATEMENT BY UNITED STATES REPRESENTATIVE ON FINAL DECLARATION AT CLOSING SESSION OF GENEVA CONFERENCE, July 21, 1954

The Chairman: I will continue calling upon countries to speak on the subject of the Declaration. I call upon the United States of America.

Mr. Bedell Smith (United States): Mr. Chairman, Fellow Delegates, as I stated to my colleagues during our meeting on July 18, my Government is not prepared to join in a Declaration by the Conference such as is submitted. However, the United States makes this unilateral declaration of its position in these matters:

The Government of the United States being resolved to devote its efforts to the strengthening of peace in accordance with the principles and purposes of the United Nations

Takes Note of the Agreements concluded at Geneva on July 20 and 21, 1954, between (a) the Franco-Laotian Command and the Command of the People's Army of Vietnam; (b) the Royal Khmer Army Command and the Command of the People's Army of Vietnam; (c) the Franco-Vietnamese Command and the Command of the People's Army of Vietnam, and of paragraphs 1 to 12 of the Declaration presented to the Geneva Conference on July 21, 1954.

The Government of the United States of America

Declares with regard to the aforesaid Agreements and paragraphs that (i) it will refrain from the threat or the use of force to disturb them, in accordance with Article 2 (Section 4) of the Charter of the United Nations dealing with the obligation of members to refrain in their international relations from the threat or use of force; and (ii) it would view any renewal of the aggression in violation of the aforesaid Agreements with grave concern and as seriously threatening international peace and security.

In connection with the statement in the Declaration concerning free election in Vietnam, my Government wishes to make clear its position which it has expressed in a Declaration made in Washington on June 29, 1954, as follows:

"In the case of nations now divided against their will, we shall continue to seek to achieve unity through free elections, supervised by the United Nations to ensure that they are conducted fairly."

With respect to the statement made by the Representative of the State of Vietnam, the United States reiterates its traditional position that peoples are entitled to determine their own future and that it will not join in an agreement which would hinder this. Nothing in its declaration just made is intended to or does indicate any departure from this traditional position.

We share the hope that the agreement will permit Cambodia, Laos and Vietnam to play their part in full independence and sovereignty, in the peaceful community of nations, and will enable the peoples of that area to determine their own future.

The Chairman: The Conference will, I think, wish to take note of the statement of the Representative of the United States of America.

Appendix V

White House Statement, February 7, 1965, Announcing Retaliatory Attacks against North Vietnam

(Released on February 7, 1965. Reproduced in Department of State Bulletin, Vol. LII, No. 1339, February 22, 1965, 238-239, under the title, "*United States and South Vietnamese Forces Launch Retaliatory Attacks Against North Vietnam.*")

On February 7, U.S. and South Vietnamese air elements were directed to launch retaliatory attacks against barracks and staging areas in the southern area of North Vietnam which intelligence has shown to be actively used by Hanoi for training and infiltration of Viet Cong personnel into South Vietnam.

Results of the attack and further operational details will be announced as soon as they are reported from the field.

Today's action by the U.S. and South Vietnamese Governments was in response to provocations ordered and directed by the Hanoi regime.

Commencing at 2 a.m. on February 7th, Saigon time (1 p.m. yesterday, eastern standard time), two South Vietnamese airfields, two U.S. barracks areas, several villages, and one town in South Vietnam were subjected to deliberate surprise attacks. Substantial casualties resulted.

Our intelligence has indicated, and this action confirms, that Hanoi has ordered a more aggressive course of action against both South Vietnamese and American installations.

Moreover, these attacks were only made possible by the continuing infiltration of personnel and equipment from North Vietnam. this infiltration markedly increased during 1964 and continues to increase.

To meet these attacks the Government of South Vietnam and the U.S. Government agreed to appropriate reprisal action against North Vietnamese targets. The President's approval of this action was given after the action was discussed with and recommended by the National Security Council last night [February 6].

Today's joint response was carefully limited to military areas which are supplying men and arms for attacks in South Vietnam. As in the case of the North Vietnamese attacks in the Gulf of Tonkin last August, the response is appropriate and fitting.

As the U.S. Government has frequently stated, we seek no wider war. whether or not this course can be maintained lies with the North Vietnamese aggressors. The key to the situation remains the cessation of infiltration from North Vietnam and the clear indication by the Hanoi regime that it is prepared to cease aggression against its neighbors.

Appendix VI

The SEATO Treaty (September 8, 1954)

(T.I.A.S. 31 70, 82-86, 209 U.N. Treaty Series 36 Ratified by the United States of America on February 4, 1955. Entered into force on February 19, 1955.)

Southeast Asia Collective Defense Treaty

The Parties to this Treaty,

Recognizing the sovereign equality of all the Parties,

Reiterating their faith in the purposes and principles set forth in the Charter of the United Nations and their desire to live in peace with all peoples and all governments,

Reaffirming that, in accordance with the Charter of the United Nations, they uphold the principle of equal rights and self-determination of peoples, and declaring that they will earnestly strive by every peaceful means to promote self-government and to secure the independence of all countries whose peoples desire it and are able to undertake its responsibilities,

Desiring to strengthen the fabric of peace and freedom and to uphold the principles of democracy, individual liberty and the rule of law, and to promote the economic well-being and development of all peoples in the treaty area,

Intending to declare publicly and formally their sense of unity, so that any potential aggressor will appreciate that the Parties stand together in the area, and

Desiring further to coordinate their efforts for collective defense for the preservation of peace and security,

Therefore agrees as follows:

Article I

The Parties undertake, as set forth in the Charter of the United Nations, to settle any international disputes in which they may be involved by peaceful means in such a manner that international peace and security and justice are not endangered, and to refrain in their international relations from the threat or use of force in any manner inconsistent with the purposes of the United Nations.

Article II

In order more effectively to achieve the objectives of this Treaty, the Parties, separately and jointly, by means of continuous and effective self-help and mutual aid will maintain and develop their individual and collective capacity to resist armed attack and to prevent and counter subversive activities directed from without against their territorial integrity and political stability.

Article III

The Parties undertake to strengthen their free institutions and to cooperate with one another in the further development of economic measures, including technical assistance, designed both to promote economic progress and social well-being and to further the individual and collective efforts of governments toward these ends.

Article IV

1. Each Party recognizes that aggression by means of armed attack in the treaty area against any of the Parties or against any State or territory which the Parties by unanimous agreement may hereafter designate, would endanger its own peace and safety, and agrees that it will in that event act to meet the common danger in accordance with its constitutional processes. Measures taken under this paragraph shall be immediately reported to the Security Council of the United Nations.

2. If, in the opinion of any of the Parties, the inviolability or the integrity of the territory or the sovereignty or political independence of any Party in the treat area or of any other State or territory to which the provisions of paragraph 1 of this Article from time to time apply is threatened in any way other than by armed attack or is affected or threatened by any fact or situation which might endanger the peace of the area, the Parties shall consult immediately in order to agree on the measures which should be taken for the common defense.

3. It is understood that no action on the territory of any State designated by unanimous agreement under paragraph 1 of this Article or on any territory so designated shall be taken except at the invitation or with the consent of the government concerned.

Article V

The Parties hereby establish a Council, on which each of them shall be represented, to consider matters concerning the implementation of this Treaty. The Council shall provide for consultation with regard to military and any other planning as the situation obtaining in the treaty area may from time to time require. The Council shall be so organized as to be able to meet at any time.

Article VI

This Treaty does not affect and shall not be interpreted as affecting in any way the rights and obligations of any of the Parties under the Charter of the United Nations or the responsibility of the United Nations for the maintenance of international peace and security. Each Party declares that none of the international engagements now in force between it and any other of the Parties or any third party is in conflict with the provisions of this Treaty, and undertakes not to enter into any international engagement in conflict with this Treaty.

Article VII

Any other State in a position to further the objectives of this Treaty and to contribute to the security of the area may, by unanimous agreement of the Parties, be invited to accede to this Treaty. Any State so invited may become a Party to the Treaty by depositing its instrument of accession with the Government of the Republic of the Philippines. The Government of the Republic of the Philippines shall inform each of the Parties of the deposit of each such instrument of accession.

Article VIII

As used in this Treaty, the "treaty area" is the general area of Southeast Asia, including also the entire territories of the Asian Parties, and the general area of the Southwest Pacific not including the Pacific area north of 21 degrees 30 minutes north latitude. The Parties may, by unanimous agreement, amend this Article to include within the treaty area the territory of any State acceding to this Treaty in accordance with Article VII or otherwise to change the treaty area.

Article IX

1. This Treaty shall be deposited in the archives of the Government of the Republic of the Philippines. Duly certified copies thereof shall be transmitted by that government to the other signatories.

2. The Treaty shall be ratified and its provisions carried out by the Parties in accordance with their respective constitutional processes. The instruments of ratification shall be deposited as soon as possible with the Government of the Republic of the Philippines, which shall notify all of the other signatories of such deposit.

3. The Treaty shall enter into force between the States which have ratified it as soon as the instruments of ratification of a majority of the signatories shall have been deposited, and shall come into effect with respect to each other State on the date of the deposit of its instrument of ratification.

Article X

This Treaty shall remain in force indefinitely, but any Party may cease to be a Party one year after its notice of denunciation has been given to the Government of the Republic of the Philippines, which shall inform the Governments of the other Parties of the deposit of each notice of denunciation.

Article XI

The English text of this Treaty is binding on the Parties, but when the Parties have agreed to the French text thereof and have so notified the Government of the Republic of the Philippines, the French text shall be equally authentic and binding on the Parties.

Understanding of the United States of America

The United States of America in executing the present Treaty does so with the understanding that its recognition of the effect of aggression and armed attack and its agreement with reference thereto in Article IV, paragraph 1, apply only to communist aggression but affirms that in the event of other aggression or armed attack it will consult under the provisions of Article IV, paragraph 2.

In WITNESS WHEREOF, the undersigned Plenipotentiaries have signed this Treaty. Done at Manila, this eighth day of September, 1954.

[signatures for Australia, France,
New Zealand, Pakistan, the Republic of
the Philippines, the Kingdom of Thailand,
the United Kingdom of Great Britain
and Northern Ireland, the United
States of America]

Protocol (September 8, 1954)

(T.I.A.S. 3170, 87. Ratified by the United States of America on February 4, 1955. Entered into force on February 19, 1955.)

Protocol to the Southeast Asia Collective Defense Treaty

Designation of States and Territory as to which provisions of Article IV and Article III are to be applicable

The Parties to the Southeast Asia Collective Defense Treaty unanimously designate for the purposes of Article IV of the Treaty the States of Cambodia and Laos and the free territory under the jurisdiction of the State of Vietnam.

The Parties further agree that the above mentioned states and territory shall be eligible in respect of the economic measures contemplated by Article III.

This Protocol shall enter into force simultaneously with the coming into force of the Treaty.

In WITNESS WHEREOF, the undersigned Plenipotentiaries have signed this Protocol to the Southeast Asia Collective Defense Treaty.

Done at Manila, this eighth day of September, 1954.

[same signatures]

Bibliography

prepared by Burns H. Weston

BOOKS

Herbert Aptheker, Staughton Lynd, Thomas Hayden, MISSION TO HANOI (New York: International Publications, 1966).

Robert McAfee Brown, Abraham J. Heschel, Michael Novak, VIETNAM: CRISIS OF CONSCIENCE (New York: Association Press, Behrman House, Herder & Herder, 1967).

Clergy and Laymen Concerned About Vietnam (Commissioned by), IN THE NAME OF AMERICA: A STUDY (New York: Clergy and Laymen Concerned About Vietnam, 1968).

Harlan Cleveland, THE OBLIGATIONS OF POWER: AMERICAN DIPLOMACY IN SEARCH FOR PEACE (New York: Harper & Row, 1966).

Theodore Draper, THE ABUSE OF POWER (New York: Viking, 1967).

Richard A. Falk (ed.), THE VIETNAM WAR AND INTERNATIONAL LAW (Princeton, New Jersey: Princeton University Press, 1968).

J. William Fulbright, THE ARROGANCE OF POWER (New York: Random House, 1967).

Marvin E. Gettleman (ed.), VIETNAM: HISTORY, DOCUMENTS AND OPINIONS ON A MAJOR WORLD CRISIS (Greenwich, Conn.: Fawcett, 1965).

Richard N. Goodwin, TRIUMPH OR TRAGEDY: REFLECTIONS ON VIETNAM (New York: Random House, 1966).

Ernest Gruening and Herbert W. Beaser, VIETNAM FOLLY (Washington, D.C.: The National Press Inc., 1967).

David Halberstam, THE MAKING OF A QUAGMIRE (New York: Random House, 1965).

Edward S. Herman and Richard B. DuBoff, AMERICA'S VIETNAM POLICY: THE STRATEGY OF DECEPTION (Washington, D.C.: Public Affairs Press, 1966).

Robert Kastenmeier, VIETNAM HEARINGS: VOICES FROM THE GRASSROOTS (New York: Doubleday, 1966).

Staughton Lynd, THE OTHER SIDE (New York: New American Library, 1967).

Mary McCarthy, VIETNAM (New York: Harcourt, Brace & World, 1967).

Hans Morgenthau, VIETNAM AND THE UNITED STATES (Washington D.C.: Public Affairs Press, 1965).

Marcus G. Raskin and Bernard B. Fall (ed.), THE VIETNAM READER (New York: Random House, 1965).

Edwin O. Reischauer, BEYOND VIETNAM: THE UNITED STATES AND ASIA (New York: Knopf, 1967).

Bertrand Russell, WAR CRIMES IN VIETNAM (New York: Monthly Review Press, 1967).

Arthur Schlesinger, Jr., THE BITTER HERITAGE: VIETNAM AND AMERICAN DEMOCRACY, 1941-1966 (Boston: Houghton, Mifflin, 1967).

Maxwell Taylor, RESPONSIBILITY AND RESPONSE (New York: Harper & Row, 1967).

United States Senate Committee on Foreign Relations, THE VIETNAM HEARINGS: WITH AN INTRODUCTION BY J. WILLIAM FULBRIGHT (New York: Random House, 1966).

Robert S. Woito (ed.), VIETNAM PEACE PROPOSALS (Berkeley, Cal.: World Without War Council of Northern California, 1967).

Howard Zinn, VIETNAM: THE LOGIC OF WITHDRAWAL (Boston: Beacon Press, 1967).

ARTICLES

Neill H. Alford, Jr., The *Legality of American Military Involvement in Vietnam: A Broader Perspective*, 72 YALE LAW JOURNAL 1109 (1966).

Comment, *The United States in Vietnam: A Case Study in the Law of Intervention*, 50 CALIFORNIA LAW REVIEW 515 (1962).

Department of State (Office of the Legal Advisor), *The Legality of United States Participation in the Defense of Vietnam*, 75 YALE LAW JOURNAL 1085 (1966).

Eberhard P. Deutsch, *The Legality of the United States Position in Vietnam*, 52 AMERICAN BAR ASSOCIATION JOURNAL 436 (1966).

Richard A. Falk, I*nternational Law and the United States' Role in the Vietnam War*, 75 YALE LAW JOURNAL 1122 (1966).

Richard A. Falk, *International Law and the United States' Role in Vietnam: A Response to Professor Moore*, 76 YALE LAW JOURNAL 1095 (1967).

Richard A. Falk, *U.S. in Vietnam: Rationale and Law* , 13 DISSENT 275 (1966).

Tom Farer, *Intervention in Civil Wars: A Modest Proposal*, 67 COLUMBIA LAW REVIEW 266 (1967).

Wolfgang Friedmann, *United States Policy and the Crisis of International Law*, 59 AMERICAN JOURNAL OF INTERNATIONAL LAW 857 (1965).

Wolfgang Friedmann, *Law and Politics in the Vietnamese War: A Comment*, 61 AMERICAN JOURNAL OF INTERNATIONAL LAW 776 (1967).

Leonard C. Meeker, *Vietnam and the International Law of Self Defense*, 56 U.S. DEPARTMENT OF STATE BULLETIN 54 (1967).

John Norton Moore, *Lawfulness of Military Assistance to the Republic of Vietnam*, 61 AMERICAN JOURNAL OF INTERNATIONAL LAW 1 (1967).

John Norton Moore and James L. Underwood, *Lawfulness of United States Assistance to the Republic of Vietnam*, 5 DUQUESNE LAW REVIEW 235 (1967).

John Norton Moore, *International Law and the United States Role in Vietnam: A Reply*, 76 YALE LAW JOURNAL 1051 (1967).

Hans Morgenthau, *To Intervene or Not to Intervene*, 45 FOREIGN AFFAIRS 425 (1967).

Note, *American Actions in Vietnam: Justifiable in International Law?*, 19 STANFORD LAW REVIEW 1307 (1967).

Daniel G. Partan, *Legal Aspects of the Vietnam Conflict*, 46 BOSTON UNIVERSITY LAW REVIEW 281 (1966).

Justus M. van der Kroef, *The United States, Vietnam & International Law*, 20 EASTERN WORLD 17 (May/June 1966).

Quincy Wright, *Legal Aspects of the Vietnam Situation*, 60 AMERICAN JOURNAL OF INTERNATIONAL LAW 750 (1966).

Index